Selling to an ESOP

Eighth Edition

Selling to an ESOP

Eighth Edition

Edited by Scott S. Rodrick

The National Center for Employee Ownership
Oakland, CA

Selling to an ESOP, 8th edition
Editing and book design by Scott S. Rodrick

Copyright © 2005 by The National Center for Employee Ownership. All rights reserved. No part of this book may be reproduced or transmitted in any form or by any means, electronic or mechanical, including photocopying, recording, or by any information storage and retrieval system, without prior written permission from the publisher.

The National Center for Employee Ownership
1736 Franklin St., 8th Flr.
Oakland, CA 94612
(510) 208-1300
Fax (510) 272-9510
E-mail *nceo@nceo.org*
Web *www.nceo.org*

First edition published 1996; second edition, 1997; third edition, 1988; fourth edition, 1999; fifth edition, 1999; sixth edition, 2000, revised printing, 2001; seventh edition, 2002; eighth edition, 2005, reprinted 2006

ISBN: 1-932924-03-5

Contents

PREFACE

Selling to employees through an employee stock ownership plan and trust (ESOP) is often the best alternative (in terms of tax, financial, and intangible benefits) for owners of closely held businesses who want to sell part or all of their companies. The alternatives to a sale to an ESOP are usually not feasible or palatable to such business owners. For example, an initial public offering (IPO) is available to only a select group of companies in the U.S. and imposes time constraints on when the owner can "sell out" after the IPO. A sale to a third party often results in protracted negotiations with someone who does not view the corporation in the same way the owner does and who has no concern for the welfare of the employees who have helped the owner increase the value of the corporation so it will be valuable to a third party.

An ESOP can provide a market for a closely held business, which can be sold to the ESOP either as a going concern or in stages. The ESOP also provides significant tax incentives for the selling shareholder, the corporation that establishes the ESOP, and the employees of the corporation. Additionally, companies that combine broad-based employee ownership (as through an ESOP) with employee participation programs tend to show substantial performance gains.

This book is designed to educate owners, managers, and advisors of closely held businesses on selling to an ESOP. The first part of the book, "Basic Considerations for Selling to an ESOP," provides general background information that will be necessary in evaluating whether an ESOP makes sense in a particular situation. The second part of the book, "Section 1042 and the ESOP Rollover," discusses in detail the main tax incentive that encourages many owners of closely held businesses to sell to an ESOP: the deferral of capital gains recognition on the sale of C corporation stock to an ESOP when the sale proceeds are "rolled over" into qualified replacement property.

Much of the material in this book originally appeared in other NCEO publications, particularly the *Journal of Employee Ownership Law and Finance,* and has been revised, expanded, and updated as needed for successive editions of this book. The *Journal* is published quarterly by the NCEO and is the only professional journal in the U.S. devoted to employee ownership.

We hope that you enjoy this book and that it inspires you to evaluate carefully the benefits of employee ownership through the use of an ESOP.

Eighth Edition (2005)

The book has been updated and reorganized where needed to reflect recent developments (as of the end of 2004) and improve the book's usefulness. Some excess material has been removed to sharpen the book's focus on its topic. Finally, the original chapter on S corporations was removed because it is now, in an expanded and revised form, a chapter in our book *S Corporation ESOPs.* Readers should refer to that book for detailed coverage of the issues pertaining to ESOPs in S corporations. That chapter has been replaced with a shorter, less technical chapter that fits in better with the scope and emphasis of this book.

INTRODUCTION

DAVID R. JOHANSON

Perhaps the most powerful tax and business succession planning tool available to shareholders of a closely held company is the ability to sell stock to a trust created pursuant to an employee stock ownership plan (ESOP) and defer or permanently avoid taxation on any gain resulting from the sale. The ESOP structure also is very powerful for the company from a tax and financial perspective because it provides for tax deductions to the company for the funds that are used to fund the purchase of company stock. An ESOP also can produce greater commitment and productivity from employees and, in turn, greater stock value, provided that employees understand how their work affects the stock value and are given an opportunity to have constructive input on their day-to-day efforts in the workplace. In order to generate these intangible benefits of broad-based employee ownership through an ESOP, employers must invest a substantial amount of time in fostering an "ownership culture" where employee owners are informed and educated about the company's finances and may give input into decisions affecting the conduct of their jobs, which can lead to a general sense of responsibility for the success of the employer's business plan, including a focus on limiting expenses, maximizing revenues, and increasing profits and value.

An example of the tax advantages available to selling shareholders and the company for a sale to an ESOP trust is instructive. A shareholder who owns stock worth $3,000,000 in a closely held company (for which stock he or she originally paid $200,000) will pay $658,000 in federal and state income taxes on the sale (assuming a combined federal and state tax rate of approximately 23.5%), meaning that he or she will net $2,342,000, at best, from the sale.

In contrast, by selling his or her stock to an ESOP, he or she will pay no federal income taxes, and possibly no state income taxes, on the sale. The selling shareholder will net $3,000,000 on the sale, a tax savings of $658,000! This tax deferral (and, possibly, complete avoidance) is available, however, only if the following requirements are satisfied:

- The selling shareholder must be either an individual, a trust, an estate, a partnership, or a limited liability company, and it must have owned the company stock sold to the ESOP trust for at least three years.

- The selling shareholder must *not* have received the stock from a qualified retirement plan (e.g., an ESOP or stock bonus plan), by exercising a stock option, or through an employee stock purchase program.

- The sale must otherwise qualify for capital gains treatment but for the sale to the ESOP trust.

- The stock sold to the ESOP trust must (in general) be voting common stock with the greatest voting and dividend rights of any class of common stock or preferred stock that is convertible into such voting common stock.

- For the 12 months preceding the sale to the ESOP trust, the company that establishes the ESOP must have had no class of stock that was readily tradable on an established securities market.

- After the sale, the ESOP trust must own at least 30% of the company that establishes the ESOP (on a fully diluted basis). Although not a requirement for the tax deferral, the company also must consent to the election of tax-deferred treatment, a 10% excise tax is imposed on the company for certain dispositions of stock by the ESOP within three years after the sale (and while the ESOP loan is outstanding, in certain circumstances), and a 50% excise tax is applied if certain prohibited persons (i.e., the selling shareholder and/or certain family members and/or more-than-25% shareholders) receive allocations of the company stock that the selling shareholder sold to the ESOP trust.

- Within a 15-month period beginning three months before the sale to the ESOP trust and ending 12 months after the sale, the selling shareholder must reinvest the sale proceeds in qualified replacement securities (QRP) (common or preferred stock, bonds, and/or debt instruments) issued by publicly traded or closely held domestic corporations that use more than 50% of their assets in an active trade or business and whose passive investment income for the preceding year did not exceed 25% of their gross receipts. Municipal bonds are not eligible reinvestment vehicles, nor are certificates of deposit issued by banks or savings and loans, mutual funds, or securities issued by the U.S. Treasury.

- The ESOP must be established in a C corporation, not an S corporation. (S corporation ESOPs do, however, have their own substantial tax advantages, discussed below.)

Many of these requirements are subject to legislative change and should be monitored carefully before the sale to an ESOP trust. In addition to these requirements for the tax deferral, the company stock purchased by the ESOP trust may not be allocated to the seller, certain members of his or her family, or any shareholder in the company that establishes the ESOP trust who owns more than 25% of any class of company stock (at any time during the one-year period ending on the date of the sale to the ESOP or the date on which "qualified securities" are allocated to ESOP participants). A prohibited allocation causes a 50% excise tax to be imposed on the company and adverse income tax consequences to the participant receiving the allocation.

The tax deferral has one downside that many selling shareholders focus on: a subsequent sale of the QRP will trigger the tax that had been deferred by the sale to the ESOP trust. To address this problem, investment alternatives have been developed and carefully and repeatedly refined in recent years.

One of a number of commercially acceptable approaches to accomplishing the tax deferral involves investment in publicly registered debt securities, issued by highly rated companies such as Dupont, Merck, United Parcel Corporation, and Minnesota Mining & Manufacturing. Morgan Stanley Dean Witter, UBS, Solomon Smith Barney, Merrill Lynch, Wachovia Securities, and other investment advisory firms have helped bring to market a number of similar securities in recent years. These floating rate note debt securities often have a maturity of 35 to 50 or more years and bear a floating-rate coupon indexed to 30-day commercial paper, LIBOR, or some other floating-rate index. These securities also normally have call protection for 30 to 50 years. These debt securities can be margined (without recourse except with respect to the securities) up to 85% to 90% or more of their market value, if properly structured, allowing investors access to a substantial portion of their initial sale proceeds to create an actively managed portfolio without triggering any tax liability on the part of the selling shareholder, without limiting the selling shareholders' reinvestment choices, and with a step-up in basis for the selling shareholders. The borrowing cost is usually the broker call loan rate (or, in recent years, a much better negotiated rate with institutional lenders such as DeutscheBank) plus a spread (in larger transactions, 45 to 80 basis points), which is greatly offset by the income earned on the floating rate note debt securities. When interest rates were substantially higher than they are today, these types of reinvestment transactions actually produced a positive spread of interest to the selling shareholders (i.e., the interest paid on the securities was greater than the borrowing cost). There are a number of traps for selling shareholders who do not properly structure their reinvestments in these securities, so caution and due diligence is warranted.

Variations of this reinvestment strategy involving the purchase of equity securities rather than floating rate debt securities also are now available. There are more investment and potential tax risks associated with this strategy; however, the potential rewards and investment returns are substantial, and the percentage of sale proceeds that must be committed to accomplish this tax deferral strategy is approximately 10%.

Careful planning of the reinvestment of the ESOP sale proceeds is extremely important. The business owner who sells his or her company to the employees through an ESOP can create liquidity today while deferring capital gains taxes potentially indefinitely (as described above). In the event of the selling shareholder's death after the ESOP sale, his or her heirs will receive a stepped-up basis on the QRP, meaning the taxation on the sale of his or her business is avoided forever. With the help of a knowledgeable investment advisor, the selling shareholder also can design a well-diversified portfolio with the monies that are not used to purchase floating rate note debt securities and/or equities that can be rebalanced according to the changing fundamental and technical conditions of the capital markets. Gifting of QRP to a charitable remainder trust (CRT) is an alternative available to selling shareholders who want to establish an actively managed portfolio without the investment and other risks associated with the margined approaches to purchasing QRP rather than buying and holding QRP in a well-diversified portfolio. If a selling shareholder has donative intent, this planning alternative has some merit. The primary drawback of this strategy is that although the selling shareholder (and his or her family) may receive the income on the QRP transferred to the CRT during the selling shareholder's lifetime, the principal will be transferred to the designated charities upon the selling shareholder's death.

In addition to the tax advantages available to the selling shareholder in a C corporation ESOP transaction, there are significant tax deductions available to the company that sponsors the ESOP. This is fundamentally as important as the tax advantages for the selling shareholder, and maybe more so for many of the ESOP transactions that occur each year.

Assuming this tax deferral/avoidance and the company tax deductions appeal to the owner of a closely held business, how does such an owner go about selling 30% or more of his or her company to an ESOP trust? The first step is a feasibility study, which tells the owner whether the characteristics of the company and his or her circumstances are such that he or she is a good candidate for a sale to an ESOP trust. This feasibility study may involve one or more conversations with a qualified employee ownership attorney or a full-blown written feasibility analysis prepared by an attorney and/or financial consultant.

If the circumstances are such that the ESOP alternative is feasible, the next key step is to obtain an independent professional valuation of the entire company and of the portion of the company that is being sold to the ESOP trust. A valuation by an independent appraiser is one of the requirements for a transaction between an ESOP trust and an owner of the company that establishes the ESOP. Under the Employee Retirement Income Security Act of 1974, as amended, and the Internal Revenue Code of 1986, as amended (the "Code"), the ESOP trust cannot pay more than fair market value for the company stock that it purchases from the selling shareholder. The independent appraisal is used by the ESOP fiduciary (a board of trustees, an administrative committee, or an institutional trustee) to ensure that the ESOP trust does not pay more than fair market value for the company stock, as determined as of the date of the sale. Based on existing case law and regulatory guidance, the ESOP fiduciary must conduct the proper due diligence to make this determination in good faith.

The ESOP plan document and the ESOP trust agreement must be designed and implemented as the valuation process progresses. If the company does not have adequate cash resources to finance the purchase of company stock by the ESOP trust, as is usually the case, the company must obtain a loan from a commercial lender or the ESOP must receive credit from the selling shareholder, and loan terms (e.g., interest rate, prepayment penalties, commitment fees, costs, restrictive covenants, and collateral) must be negotiated. In addition, a stock purchase agreement between the owner of the company and the ESOP trust must be negotiated and prepared.

The ESOP trust then typically borrows the money from the company, which, in turn, borrows from a commercial lender, or the ESOP receives credit from the selling shareholder to purchase the company stock. The ESOP trust uses these loan proceeds or credit to purchase company stock from the owner at no more than its fair market value, as determined by an independent appraiser and confirmed in good faith by the ESOP fiduciary as of the date of the purchase.

The company's debt to the commercial lender and the ESOP's debt to the company are normally repaid over a five- to ten-year term (or even more) with tax-deductible contributions by the company to the ESOP trust. The company, the ESOP trust, and the selling shareholders should work together to obtain the best terms possible for such financing. Collateral, corporate governance, and personal guarantees (or the lack thereof) are often issues on which the parties may have differences that need to be resolved. Contributions used to repay ESOP loan principal are generally deductible up to an amount equal to 25% of the total compensation paid or accrued to all participating employees. (Please see the relevant discussion in this book's chapter on contribution and allocation limits.) "Compensation" for this purpose includes wages that an employee elects to defer pursuant to a cash-or-deferred arrangement under a 401(k) plan. Furthermore, the 25% limit does not include salary reduction contributions to a 401(k) plan. In other words, an employer may contribute 25% of the total compensation paid or accrued to all participating employees in order for an ESOP to repay loan principal in addition to salary reduction contributions, provided that the annual addition limitation of $41,000 (as indexed for inflation) for individual ESOP participants is not exceeded.

In a C corporation ESOP, contributions to the ESOP trust that are used to pay the interest on the ESOP's loan from the company are fully deductible, and they are not included in the 25% contribution limit so long as not more than one-third of the contributions are used to repay principal and interest and allocated to "highly compensated employees."

In a C corporation, reasonable cash dividends on ESOP-trust held company stock also are deductible and not included in the 25% contribution limit if they are passed through directly to ESOP participants, used to repay a leveraged ESOP's loan, or are reinvested in company stock at the direction of participants instead of being passed through to them. The timing of the dividend deduction differs depending upon whether the dividends are (1) paid or distributed to the ESOP participant, (2) reinvested in company stock, or (3) are used to repay a leveraged ESOP's loan. With respect to dividends described in (1), the deduction is allowable in the C corporation's taxable year in which the dividends are paid or distributed to an ESOP participant or his or her beneficiary. With respect to dividends described in (2), the law that makes these types of dividends deductible includes a technical error (a prior reference for the timing of the deduction for dividends described in (3) incorrectly refers to the dividends described in (2)) that does not make it clear when the deduction is allowable. Intuitively, the dividend should be allowable in the C corporation's taxable year in which the dividends would have been distributed to ESOP participants and instead were reinvested in company stock at the direction of such participants. With respect to dividends described in (3), the deduction is allowable in the C corporation's taxable year in which they are used to repay the leveraged ESOP's loan.

In S corporations, distributions on ESOP-held company stock are not deductible; however, based upon a provision in the American Jobs Creation Act of 2004 that was signed into law on October 22, 2004, distributions on both allocated and unallocated shares of company stock held by the ESOP may be used to repay an ESOP loan. This new law is retroactively effective back to January 1, 1998. The exact details of such retroactivity will be worked out in the future through regulations and/or regulatory interpretations, etc. It appears that distributions of earnings to an S corporation ESOP may not be passed through to ESOP participants, based on an express denial of a private letter ruling request in 1999 (that would have allowed such pass-through distributions) and on a dearth of statutory and/or regulatory support in the Code. To the extent distributions of S corporation ESOP earnings are not or may not be used to repay an ESOP loan, they may be used for ESOP distribution purposes.

Under current law, as enacted in 1997 for years beginning on or after January 1, 1998, S corporation ESOPs are exempt from the unrelated business income tax (UBIT); thus, if an ESOP trust owns all of an S corporation's issued and outstanding capital stock, no current tax is imposed on the company's income. (That income is eventually taxed because ESOP participants in S corporations are taxed on ESOP distributions, just as C corporation ESOP participants are.) The Economic Growth and Tax Relief Reconciliation Act of 2001, as amended (the "2001 Act"), which the President signed into law on June 7, 2001, restricts the abuse of this provision by plans designed to benefit only a small number of employees, whether in a very small company or where a small number of employees try to set up an S corporation ESOP just for their own benefit while operating a larger company whose employees are not in the ESOP.

The ESOP community strongly supported the anti-abuse S corporation restriction in the Act. In fact, the 2001 Act, which includes H.R. 10 and S.742, the Portman-Cardin and Grassley-Baucus bills, is landmark legislation for ESOPs, and no prior legislation in U.S. history has been as positive for retirement plans governed by ERISA, including ESOPs. The 1984 and 1986 tax bills, under the guidance of former Senator Russell Long (the first and possibly the strongest-ever ESOP advocate in Congress) and the National Center for Employee Ownership's executive director, Corey Rosen, among many others, included the most advantageous specific ESOP legislation ever passed. Those bills, however, included many cutbacks in retirement plan incentives for defined contribution plans in general.

The 2001 Act also included the first expansion of an ESOP tax incentive for a C corporation (expansion of the deduction for reinvested dividends paid on company stock held by an ESOP) enacted by Congress in 15 years. The 2001 Act solidified the legislative environment for S corporation ESOPs and helped ensure this significant tax incentive for ESOPs will make them attractive to a growing number of companies. This legislation also made funding defined contribution plans more flexible and attractive to employers and permits substantially more dollars to be added to rank-and-file employees' retirement plan accounts. Current proposed tax legislation from both the U.S. House of Representatives and the U.S. Senate include a number of very positive legislative provisions for ESOPs and the corporations that sponsor ESOPs.

An ESOP is a versatile financial and motivational tool that can be used by a selling shareholder and a company to obtain significant tax benefits in selling a portion or all of his or her company. An ESOP also can be used in connection with the spinoff of a division or corporate expansion or as an acquisition planning tool; it can be given a special class of preferred stock to minimize equity dilution; and it can be combined with a 401(k) plan to attract employee equity into a company. For both financial and non-financial reasons, selling stock to an ESOP should be irresistible to many closely held companies and their shareholders.

PART 1

BASIC CONSIDERATIONS FOR SELLING TO AN ESOP

1

AN INTRODUCTION TO ESOPs

COREY ROSEN

Some years ago, employee stock ownership plans (ESOPs) were just another wallflower in the Internal Revenue Code, appealing only to a small, but smitten, coterie of professionals and a growing number of mostly private companies. True, ESOPs were piling up some impressive numbers—about 500 new plans a year, adding about 500,000 to 1,000,000 new employees annually. There were occasional splashes of media attention, especially in those rare cases when employees used an ESOP to save a failing company. But in recent years, ESOPs have lost their obscurity and perhaps their innocence as well. ESOPs were used to buy major companies, many with several thousand or more employees. Public companies, who once scorned ESOPs as unattractive, suddenly rushed to embrace them, borrowing billions of dollars to make employees shareholders. Lenders, investment bankers, and other Wall Street denizens came courting as well, finding hidden beauty in ESOP tax breaks. Basking in the glow of all this new attention, ESOP borrowing soared from just $1.2 billion in 1986 to over $24 billion in 1989 alone. The recession of 1990–1993 cooled this trend, but ESOPs regained momentum with the following economic upturn. As of 2004, there are roughly 11,000 ESOPs, covering over 9 million employees.

Now that ESOPs have become a center of attention, they are also the subject of much greater scrutiny. Are they really a means to create a more equitable distribution of wealth, as Congress intended? Do they actually increase corporate performance, as many ESOP promoters believe? Are they appropriate for every company? Or are they just another elaborate tax dodge benefiting managers and investment bankers more than employees?

Overall, ESOPs do, in fact, seem to be performing well. They often provide employees with substantial capital ownership, and they can help a company perform much better. For many companies, an ESOP is an ideal solution to problems of business continuity, employee benefit planning, or raising capital. But the beauty of ESOPs is largely a reflection of the motives and practices of the companies that embrace them. When paired with participative management practices and a corporate philosophy stressing the centrality of ownership, they shine. When partnered only with a desire to capture the fleeting glory of the moment's tax breaks, they quickly fade into little more than a public subsidy of financial cleverness.

Rules and Regulations

Before evaluating how ESOPs are working and what makes them work best, first we need to explore what they are and what they do.

An ESOP is a defined contribution employee benefit plan, technically a stock bonus plan that can borrow money. ESOPs can be used for a variety of purposes and can give employees anywhere from 1% to 100% ownership of a company. The NCEO estimates that about a third of all ESOPs own or will own a majority of the stock and that the typical plan initially is designed to own about 30% to 40%. ESOPs can be found in every size and kind of company, from small retailers to industrial giants.

Contrary to popular impression, ESOPs are only rarely used to save failing firms, such as at the widely publicized Weirton Steel Corporation near Pittsburgh, or to prevent hostile takeovers, such as the ESOP at Lockheed. The NCEO estimates that fewer than 1% of all ESOPs are set up for these two purposes. Moreover, according to the U.S. General Accounting Office (GAO), only 3% of all ESOPs require employee concessions. The GAO also found only 8% of all ESOPs are set up in place of pension plans, while Douglas Kruse at Rutgers University found ESOP companies overall are much more likely to offer 401(k), pension, and profit sharing plans than comparable non-ESOP companies. In this sense, such ESOPs present a much more solid base for retirement than the plans of Enron and some other public companies that focused their 401(k) plans on company stock.

✔ **Setting Up an ESOP**   To establish an ESOP, a company sets up a trust fund, into which it contributes new shares of its own stock or cash to buy existing shares. Alternatively, the ESOP can borrow money to buy new or existing shares, with the company making cash contributions to the plan to enable it to repay the loan. Regardless of how the plan acquires stock, company contributions to the trust are tax-deductible, generally up to 25% of covered pay.

ESOPs are governed by detailed rules designed to ensure employee participants are treated fairly. Shares in the ESOP trust must be allocated to individual employee accounts. Normally, all full-time employees over 21 with at least 1,000 hours of service in a year participate in the plan, although a company can exclude employees covered by a collective bargaining agreement (provided it bargains in good faith about whether these employees will be included). In some cases, however, ESOPs can include only employees in a certain line of business of the company, provided the effect is not to discriminate in favor of higher-paid people (such as making the managers a separate division). ESOPs can also base participation on matches of employee contributions to a savings plan such as a 401(k) plan, provided certain complex rules assuring equitable participation by lower-paid employees are met.

Allocations are made either on the basis of relative pay or under some more equal formula. As employees accumulate seniority with the firm, they acquire an increasing right to the shares in their accounts, a process known as "vesting." Stock must either be 100% vested after five years, or must start vesting at 20% per year after three years until full vesting occurs at seven years. If an ESOP is used to match 401(k) deferrals, vesting cannot occur over more than six years.

In a leveraged plan, the ESOP holds the shares in a "suspense account." Each year, as the loan is repaid, a percentage of the shares in the account equal to the percentage of the loan repaid is released to employee accounts.

The ESOP trust is governed by a trustee, usually appointed by management. The trustee can be an "insider," such as a company officer, or an "outsider," such as a bank trust department. The trustee oversees the ESOP to ensure it operates for "the exclusive benefit of the employees." Because of this legal responsibility, some ESOP experts advise that it is safer to have an outside, independent trustee.

In private companies, employees must be able to vote their allocated shares on major issues, such as closing or relocating, but the company can choose to pass through voting rights (such as for the board of directors) on other issues. If the employees do not vote the shares, management usually directs the ESOP trustee as to how the shares should be voted. In public companies, employees must be able to vote on all issues.

✔ **When Employees Leave** When employees leave the firm, they receive their stock, which the company must buy back from them at its fair market value (unless there is a public market for the shares). Private companies must have an annual outside valuation to determine the value of their shares. All ESOP transactions must take place at this appraised value. Valuations are normally done annually (more often if there are interim major transactions) and assess such things as earnings capacity, hard assets, goodwill, market and industry conditions, and other factors that determine a business' worth. Companies can distribute the ESOP accounts all at once or in equal installments over up to five years. For employees who leave due to death, retirement, or disability, payment must start within a year. For those leaving earlier, companies can wait up to six years, or until the ESOP loan is repaid, if that is longer.

✔ **Military Leave** In the case of employees on military leave, employers must comply with the Uniformed Services Employment and Reemployment Rights Act (USERRA). By law, for all retirement plan benefits, employees must continue to receive vesting as if they still worked for the company.

There is no break in service. Employers are not required to make contributions or allocate forfeitures during the time of service, however. If there is a 401(k) plan, the employee has the right, over the lesser of five years or three times the length of employment, to make make-up contributions, and the employer would have to match these according to the formula that otherwise would have applied.

Uses of ESOPs

✔ **Tax Benefits** ESOPs can be used in a number of tax-advantaged ways. When the ESOP does not borrow money, contributions of stock or cash to buy stock are deductible up to 25% of the payroll of the plan's participants. The size of contributions is at the company's discretion. If the ESOP borrows money, the principal portion of the loan is deductible up to 25% of the annual payroll of plan participants. All the interest is deductible as well, provided no more than one-third of the ESOP benefits go to "highly compensated" people. Dividends on ESOP shares passed through to participants are tax-deductible to the company. So are dividends used to repay an ESOP loan. Moreover, dividends used to repay a loan do not count towards the 25%-of-pay limits.

In all these cases, there is a maximum annual addition to an employee's account of the lesser of 100% of pay or $41,000 (as of 2004; the dollar figure is indexed for inflation). Pay over $205,000 per year (as of 2004; this too is indexed for inflation) is not counted in making contributions. As with total pay, however, dividends on the ESOP loan paid to participants do not count toward these limits.

These deductions can be combined with other ESOP tax benefits to provide a variety of attractive uses for ESOPs.

✔ **Buying the Shares of a Departing Owner** Owners of privately held corporations can use an ESOP to create a ready market for their shares. Under this approach, the company can make tax-deductible cash contributions to the ESOP to buy out an owner's shares, or it can have the ESOP borrow money to buy the shares (see below). If the company is a C corporation, once the ESOP owns 30% or more of all the shares in the company, the seller can "roll over" (reinvest) the proceeds of the sale in the securities (stocks, bonds, debentures, etc.) of other domestic operating companies and defer any tax on the gain, provided certain rules are followed. This benefit applies only to sellers who have held the stock for three years before the sale.

Using an ESOP to buy out an owner, of course, will work only in a company with earnings adequate to buy the owner's equity. The price of that equity must be determined by an outside valuation.

About half of all ESOPs are set up to buy out an owner in this way. This use of ESOPs is one that almost always is "win-win." Many profitable, closely held businesses are difficult to sell and end up being liquidated; many others are sold to competitors or investors more interested in their markets, technologies, or assets than in keeping them open. In most of these cases, an ESOP would at least be a realistic option. By selling to an ESOP, jobs are retained and capital ownership is spread.

The ESOP does not have to buy the whole business, of course. It can also purchase the shares of minority owners, or just part of the shares of a principal owner. An ESOP might buy 30% of the stock in an initial leveraged transaction, for instance, then buy more shares over time with contributions from earnings or a second loan.

The mechanism to purchase the shares can be borrowing, periodic cash contributions, or seller financing (such as an installment sale). Note that if the tax-deferred rollover treatment described above is chosen, children, siblings, spouses and parents, as well as any shareholder-employees owning more than 25% of company stock, cannot receive an allocation of shares in the ESOP *on those "rolled-over" shares.* They can get allocations, however, from shares contributed to the ESOP not subject to the rollover.

✔ **Borrowing Money at a Lower After-Tax Cost**   When an ESOP borrows money, it can buy new or existing company shares. The company then makes tax-deductible contributions to the ESOP to repay the loan, meaning both principal and interest are deductible. By having the ESOP buy new shares, the company can finance new capital, acquisitions of other firms, or other growth. Or the ESOP can simply buy existing shares. As noted earlier, dividends paid on ESOP shares can be used to repay the loan as well, and any dividends paid are counted over and above the 25%-of-pay limitation. About two-thirds of all ESOPs use the leveraging feature.

The loans do not have to come from commercial lenders. Sellers can make the loan, for instance, provided they do so on an arm's length basis.

While the loan can be used for any business purpose, one of the intriguing uses of ESOPs is to fund capital improvements. A company that needs to buy trucks, buildings, machines, land, or whatever else it needs can issue new shares of stock and sell them to the ESOP, which buys them with the proceeds of the loan. The company then repays the loan in pretax dollars, and the same dollars used to make the capital investment fund an employee benefit plan. The downside of this is that the new shares dilute the ownership interests of other owners. This should only be a problem, however, if the new investment does not pay for itself. If it does, the owners will simply own a smaller piece of a larger pie.

✔ **Creating an Additional Employee Benefit** A company can simply issue new or treasury shares to an ESOP, or contribute cash, deducting the value of the contributions for up to 25% of covered pay. Employer contributions to other benefit plans, including profit sharing and pension plans, will lower this maximum level, however. Contributing to an ESOP this way means that employees get a benefit at no up-front cash cost to the company. Or a company can contribute cash, buying shares from existing public or private owners. While almost all ESOP company executives say that creating an additional employee benefit is one reason they set up their plan, the NCEO estimates that only about one-third of all ESOPs are set up primarily for this purpose.

✔ **As Part of a Leveraged Buyout** ESOPs have had considerable success as a strategy for leveraged buyouts (LBOs), typically of companies being divested from a parent firm. Sometimes these companies are in financial difficulty, but most of the time the parent simply no longer wants to be in that business. Less often, ESOPs are part of a leveraged buyout of a public firm. ESOP tax advantages are important in LBOs because of the high debt service LBOs require. They can also be an important part of the new firm's business strategy. Getting employees more involved and motivated may be critical to a company's success when so many dollars go to repaying a loan.

In the case of troubled companies, ESOPs can be an alternative, but only under certain conditions. Some companies are closed because while they are making profits, they are not profitable enough. Others are losing money because of poor labor-management relations, or because of business strategies that are inappropriate to the market. All of these present possibilities for employee buyouts. Employee ownership may provide the needed extra incentives, and the managerial freedom, for employees to create a better business. Other companies close because the market is saturated, because competition can do the same thing for much less, because they need massive infusions of new capital, or other similar structural factors. These are rarely good buyout candidates.

In the more common case of divestitures of successful firms, the ESOP faces a simpler task. Many companies are sold because the parent needs the cash, loses interest in the market, or is required to do so by antitrust rules. These companies often make excellent ESOP candidates, provided the ESOP can offer enough to outbid competitors.

In any leveraged buyout, the ESOP will rarely get 100% ownership. Typically, lenders will want to see some equity in the transaction, and key management people will want a substantial ownership interest themselves. Determining just how much equity should be offered to investors and managers, and at what price, is a complicated and often controversial issue.

ESOPs and Employee Motivation

During the early 1980s, the NCEO surveyed over 3,500 employee owners in 45 companies. We looked at hundreds of factors in an effort to determine whether it mattered to employees that they had stock in their company, and if so, when.

The results were very clear. Employees liked being owners. The more shares they owned, the more committed they were to their company, the more satisfied they were with their jobs, and the less likely they were to leave. Naturally, some employees in some companies liked being owners more than others. More than any other factor, individual employee response to ownership was a response to how much stock they got each year. After that, employees responded more favorably if they had ample opportunities to participate in decisions affecting their jobs, worked in companies whose management really believed in the concept of ownership (not just the tax breaks), and were provided regular information about how the ESOP operated.

By contrast, the size of the company, line of business, demographic characteristics of the employees, seniority, job classification, presence or absence of voting rights or board membership, percentage of the company owned by employees (as opposed to the size of the annual contribution), and many other factors did not have any impact. Employees looked at the ESOP and asked, "How much money will I get from this?" and "Am I really treated like an owner?" If they liked the answers to these questions, they liked being an owner.

Ownership and Corporate Performance

Knowing the answer to whether ESOPs motivate employees would seem to provide the answer to whether ownership improves corporate performance. Not so. In most companies, labor costs are under 30% to 40% of total costs. Motivation on its own, presumably, makes employees work harder. We at the NCEO often ask managers just how much more work they think they could hope to get from more motivated employees, based on an eight-hour day. Thirty minutes is a typical response. That comes to just 7% more time. Seven percent times even a high estimate of 40% for labor costs results in just a 2.8% savings.

That can be a lot of money, but it is not what distinguishes the really successful companies from the mediocre ones. The star performers are those that react to their environment in creative, innovative ways, providing better value to customers than their competitors. How is that achieved? Through processing information and acting on it intelligently. In most companies, the information gathering is limited to a group of managers. The generation of ideas is similarly limited. So is the decision making. The assumption is that only these people have the talent, and perhaps the motivation, to carry out these tasks.

In fact, no one has more daily contact with customers than employees, at least in most companies. No one is closer to the day-to-day process of making products or providing services than employees. Consequently, employees often have useful ideas they could share with management.

Thus, for a company to use employee ownership effectively, it needs to do more than motivate people to work harder at what, after all, may not be the most efficient or effective thing to do. Instead, it needs to enlist employee ideas and information to find the best ways to do the most important things. To do that, companies need to get employees involved. Managers should seek their opinions. Employee task forces, ad hoc and permanent, should be established to solve problems. Quality circles and employee involvement teams can be set up. Individual jobs can be enhanced and supervision limited. Suggestion systems can be implemented. This all may seem like common sense, and it is. It is not a very common practice in most companies, however.

The structure of participation varies from firm to firm, but basically boils down to employees forming groups to share information, generate ideas, and make recommendations.

At Phelps County Bank in Rolla, Missouri, the ESOP was at first a sleepy benefit plan. Then Emma Lou Brent, the bank's CEO, read that for an ESOP to work, employees must receive substantial annual contributions and have a chance to share their ideas and information on a regular basis. So Brent increased the ESOP contribution to 25% of pay per year and started an employee involvement program based on a "problem-buster committee." Employees formed a committee to solicit input on what issues were causing difficulties. Brightly colored "problem alerts" were then circulated to ask for ideas on how to solve them. Often, the solution was to form an ad hoc team of people who thought they had something to contribute. The system has grown over the years and now includes extensive training in bank management for all employees. The result is that the company's stock has gone up much faster than the increase in costs; in fact, Phelps has been one of the best-performing banks in its class for years.

At Stone Construction Equipment Company in Honoeye, New York, an ESOP set up in the late 1970s was having little effect. Then the company hired a new president, Bob Fien, who started a participative management program. Eventually, all employees were trained in "just-in-time" management and organized into work cells that schedule and control their own work flow and have considerable input into the design and organization of their jobs. Previously, Stone had been limping along and had developed a reputation for poor quality; by 1991, however, the company had made so much progress *Industry Week* named it one of America's top 10 manufacturers.

At Springfield ReManufacturing in Springfield, Missouri, employee owners are taught to read detailed financial and production data. Meeting in work groups, they go over the numbers and then figure out ways to improve them. Employees are given monthly 110-page financial statements to digest. A waste of time? Springfield's stock went from 10¢ a share when it started its ESOP in the early 1980s to $81.60 in a recent valuation. Employment is up from 130 to 1,000. Lehrer and others have featured the company.

Other approaches include employee advisory committees to management, eliminating levels of supervision while giving nonmanagement employees more authority, meetings between management and randomly selected groups of employees, suggestion boxes, and anything else companies can imagine to get people involved.

None of this is easy to do, but the results consistently have demonstrated the worth of the effort. As a result, participative management has become the hottest topic in ESOPs. Not a conference goes by without repeated imprecations, from consultants and experienced companies alike, to get moving in this area.

S Corporations and ESOPs

Historically, an S corporation could not have an ESOP that owns stock in the company (it *could* set up an ESOP, initially funding it with cash, and then become a C corporation when the ESOP acquired company stock). However, since January 1, 1998, an S corporation can now have an ESOP that owns stock in the company. Tax law changes in 1996 and 1997 made this possible, first by allowing ESOPs and certain other nontaxable trusts to own shares in S corporations, provided they pay tax on profits attributable to them as unrelated business income. The 1996 law, however, allowed employees to receive a distribution of their shares when they leave the company. That could lead to a disqualification of the company's S status if the employees rolled the stock into an IRA or if the number of shareholders exceeded 75 (the maximum number of shareholders for an S corporation at that time; for tax years beginning after 2004, the limit is now 100).

In 1997, Congress changed the law to allow S corporations to require that employees take the cash equivalent value of their shares when they receive their distributions. Certain other technical problems were fixed as well. More important, the law specifically and exclusively exempts ESOPs from the unrelated business income tax (UBIT). In other words, whatever percentage of the company the ESOP owns is not subject to any current taxation. Thus, when the ESOP owns 100% of the S corporation, which now is very common, there is no federal, and often no state, income tax.

On the other hand, the law does not provide S corporation ESOPs with the same tax benefits available to C corporation ESOPs. Specifically, (1) owners of S corporation stock cannot use the tax-deferred rollover when selling to an ESOP, (2) dividends (i.e., S corporation "distributions") used to repay a loan or passed through to participants are not deductible, and (3) interest payments on an ESOP loan count toward the contribution limits. Moreover, while contribution limits are set 25% for principal payments on an ESOP loan, interest payments and forfeitures count toward this limit.

As described in this book's chapter on S corporations, S corporation ESOPs cannot be designed just to benefit a small number of employees.

Costs, Drawbacks, and Considerations

ESOPs are expensive. Typical start-up costs for a small to medium-sized company are about $30,000 for legal, financial, and valuation work. Other services, such as an employee communication program, are additional. These costs can increase substantially if an investment banker is needed to help raise money, if there are special legal complications (such as other plans to be rolled over or terminated), or if specialized financial advice is required.

While these costs are substantial, keep in mind that selling a business (often an ESOP goal) can cost much more, with business brokers often charging a percentage of the deal, and that other employee benefit plans also require specialized legal and financial advice.

Another major consideration is the repurchase obligation. Unless a company is publicly traded, it must repurchase shares of departing employees. The more successful the company is, the more this will cost. When calculating the benefits of an ESOP, calculate as well how much will be needed to fund an adequate repurchase obligation program (your plan administrator should be able to help you do this). You must be able to fund *both* your ESOP contributions *and* your repurchase obligation.

The practicality of an ESOP also depends on your payroll base. Some companies find that the size of their payroll, relative to the amount of stock they want to buy, is too small to fall within the deduction limits. In some cases, there may be ways to get around these limits (such as by arranging for a loan with a balloon payment at the end, to be refinanced with a second loan), but often there is not.

The company's profits and cash flow may also be limiting factors. Remember that a tax deduction is not worth much if your company is not making a profit. Even if you are, you need to assess whether earnings and cash flow are sufficient to meet the projected needs of the ESOP.

Finally, the ESOP must be consistent with the organization's overall goals. Are there relatives or key employees that current owners really want to see own the firm, rather than the ESOP? Is management ready to treat employees like part owners? Does management want to encourage employees to stay with the company or would it prefer high turnover (some companies do, largely to keep benefit costs down)? Will the ESOP complement other benefit plans? If it is the only benefit plan, is it secure enough to be promoted as a "retirement" plan? In short, do the current owners and existing management really want to share ownership? If the answer is "no," ESOP specialists agree that no matter what tax gains can be made, an ESOP is probably not the best approach.

Steps to Setting Up an ESOP

If you have decided an ESOP is worth investigating, there are several steps to take to implement a plan. At each point, you may decide that you have gone far enough and that an ESOP is not right for you.

1. *Determine whether other owners are amenable.* This may seem like an obvious issue, but sometimes people take several of the steps listed below before finding out whether the existing owners are willing to sell. Employees should not start organizing a buyout unless they have some reason to think the parent firm is willing to sell (it may not be, for instance, if its goal is to reduce total output of a product it makes at other locations). Or there may be other owners of a private firm who will never agree to an ESOP, even if it seems appealing to the principal owners. They could cause a good deal of trouble down the road.

2. *Conduct a feasibility study.* This may be a full-blown analysis by an outside consultant, replete with market surveys, management interviews, and detailed financial projections,

or it may simply be a careful business plan performed in-house. Generally, full-scale feasibility studies are needed only where there is some doubt about the ESOP's ability to repay the loan. Any analysis, however, must look at several items. First, it must assess just how much extra cash flow the company has available to devote to the ESOP and whether this is adequate for the purposes for which the ESOP is intended. Second, it must determine whether the company has adequate payroll for ESOP participants to make the ESOP contributions deductible. Remember to include the effect of other benefit plans that will be maintained in these calculations. Third, estimates must be made of what the repurchase obligation will be and how the company will handle it.

3. ***Conduct a valuation.*** The feasibility study will rely on rough estimates of the value of the stock for the purpose of calculating the adequacy of cash and payroll. In public companies, of course, these estimates will be fairly accurate because they can be based on past price performance. In private companies, they will be more speculative. The next step for private firms (and some public companies as well) is a valuation. A company may want to have a preliminary valuation done first to see if the range of values produced is acceptable. A full valuation would follow if it is.

    Doing a valuation before implementing a plan is a critical step. If the value is too low, sellers may not be willing to sell. Alternatively, the price of the shares may be too high for the company to afford. The valuation consultant will look at a variety of factors, including cash flow, profits, market conditions, assets, comparable company values, goodwill, and overall economic factors. A discount on value may be taken if the ESOP is buying less than 50% of the shares. The process is described in more detail later in this book.

4. ***Hire an ESOP attorney.*** If the first three steps prove positive, the plan can now be drafted and submitted to the IRS. You should carefully evaluate your options and tell your attorney just how you want the ESOP to be set up. This could save you a great amount of money in consultation time. The IRS

may take many months to issue you a "letter of determination" on your plan, but you can go ahead and start making contributions before then. If the IRS rules unfavorably, which rarely happens, normally you just need to amend your plan.

5. ***Obtain funding for the plan.*** There are several potential sources of funding. Obviously, the ESOP can borrow money. Banks are generally receptive to ESOP loans, but, as with any loan, it makes sense to shop around. Sellers or other private parties can also make loans. Larger ESOP transactions can tap the bond market or borrow from insurance companies.

   Another source of funding is ongoing company contributions, aside from loan repayments. While ESOPs must, by law, invest primarily in employer securities, most ESOP experts believe they can temporarily invest primarily in other assets while building up a fund to buy out an owner.

   A third source is existing benefit plans. Pension plans are not a practical source of funding, but profit sharing plans are sometimes used. Profit sharing assets are simply transferred in whole or part into an ESOP. Many ESOP companies do this, but it must be done cautiously. If employees are given no choice in the switch, trustees of the plan must be able to demonstrate that the investment in company stock was prudent; if they are given a choice, there could be a securities law issue.

   Finally, employees can contribute to the plan, most commonly by wage or benefit concessions. Most ESOPs do not require these, but they are necessary in some cases. Clearly, this is an issue that must be handled very carefully.

6. ***Establish a process to operate the plan.*** A trustee must be chosen to oversee the plan. In most private companies, this will be someone from inside the firm, but some private and most public companies hire an outside trustee. An ESOP committee will direct the trustee. In most companies, this is made up of management people, but many ESOP companies allow at least some nonmanagement representation. Finally, and most importantly, a process must be established to communicate how the plan works to employees and to get them more involved as owners.

Conclusion

Employee ownership is not a panacea. A significant number of plans provide only modest, or no, net benefits to employees. Nor does employee ownership automatically improve performance. That takes considerable work and effort. Employee ownership is an even further cry from what its critics proclaim, however. It is not mostly about takeover defenses, nor does it usually require employees to give up pensions or wages to participate. Compared to most of the fixes for the economy, such as investment tax credits, research credits, industrial policy, safe-harbor leasing, and one management fad after another, employee ownership seems to be a permanent and important change in how we approach business (and one much less costly to the taxpayer). Many foreign countries, from Poland to Russia to the United Kingdom to Canada, are working to accommodate their laws to employee ownership. With all its admitted faults, it is the only idea on the horizon that combines the ideals of social equity with the promise of economic efficiency. That alone makes it worth every penny we put into it.

2

LENDING CONSIDERATIONS FOR ESOPS

DONALD DAVIS

When asked to review an ESOP loan request, the first issue for a lender is "is it creditworthy?" Would the lender make a "straight" loan to this borrower with comparable use of proceeds, maturity, and repayment terms? The classic formula is "cash flow, collateral, and character." Is there sufficient cash flow to pay back the loan? If the cash flow turns out to be deficient, is there sufficient collateral for the lender to recover its principal? Is the character of the borrower the sort you wish to do business with? This is no different for an ESOP loan. The lender will evaluate the stability of the company's net cash flow based upon such factors as the industry (including the current state and outlook of the industry), the company's competitive strengths and weaknesses, and the company's track record. Credit analysis will also include an evaluation of management and an evaluation of asset values and marketability as secondary support. In leveraged situations, a very detailed credit and cash flow analysis is prepared, due to the tight cash flow cushion inherent in greater leverage and required debt service.

Leveraged buyouts (LBOs) incorporating an ESOP have certain advantages over those without one. The first advantage is that up to 100% of the principal portion of the ESOP loan may be effectively tax-deductible, which enhances the cash flow as compared to a direct corporate loan. The increased cash flow available for additional debt service could therefore increase the amount of debt a financial institution might lend. This is where an experienced and credible ESOP advisor can be of critical support to the process. Lenders will look to the financial advisor (as well as to the ESOP attorney) to provide analysis of the tax aspects of the cash flow projections. The second advantage is that the securities portfolio created by the seller's proceeds to satisfy the requirements of a capital gains deferral under Section 1042 of the Internal Revenue Code will be "conveniently available" to provide collateral support to a seller's guarantee of the loan. These advantages may allow certain companies to withstand more leverage than a traditional leveraged loan.

Finally, an ESOP loan adds several questions to the usual loan process:

- What percentage of the company will the ESOP own?
- What tax benefits will the ESOP add to the cash flows?
- Who is the financial advisor working with the company on ESOP issues?
- Who will ongoing management be?
- What credit support can the selling owners provide?

Credit Consideration Basics

✔ **Due Diligence Preparation**   As with a non-ESOP loan, a potential ESOP lender will require the borrower to supply, as a minimum, historical financial statements, details of the use of proceeds, several years of financial projections, and details of management backgrounds. The borrower should be prepared for management discussions, reviews of the industry and competitive environment, company plant and facility tours, computer or production systems reviews, an environmental review, and other general due diligence. Depending on the nature of the audit of the financial statements, prior-year tax returns may also be required. If owner guarantees are involved, prior-year tax returns of the owner may also be required.

✔ **Management** An ESOP loan will transfer some percentage of ownership of the company. It may or may not result in a change in management. Lenders are always very concerned about management issues. Typical "due diligence" questions include the following. Who has been responsible for the past management of the company? Who will be managing the company in the future? What is their experience and track record? How have they responded to past downturns in the industry? What succession plans are there? While these are brief questions, they are absolutely crucial.

✔ **Industry and Competitive Analysis** A significant part of the borrowing package should be devoted to the borrower's perspective on this and the borrower's competitive position. What are the forces affecting the industry, and how is the industry changing? How is the borrower prepared to react to changes? Are there technological changes occurring? Are there substitute products or new competitors? How does the industry respond in a recession? These issues will drive the analysis and documentation of the projections.

✔ **Preparation of Projections** Along with its financial advisor, the borrower will be expected to provide projections, with explanations of each of the key assumptions. These should be tied to the industry and competitive analysis. Many borrowers provide only a "base case." Lenders will build their own models of the projections, and develop "sensitivity analyses." These are alternate scenarios in which specific assumptions are stressed to examine their impact on the ability of the borrower to generate sufficient cash flow to repay debt.

One sensitivity approach would be to create a "downside breakeven" case. In this approach, the assumptions are stressed until the cash flows are only at the breakeven level. Does breakeven occur at a 2% decline in sales, or does it take a 25% decline? Does breakeven occur at a 5% decline in gross margins, or does it take a 30% decline? This approach will give both the lender and the borrower a sense of how much cushion exists in the "base case" as each has separately defined it. This sensitivity is then compared to the historic volatility of the company and the industry. It is also a very useful tool for creating loan covenant levels and for monitoring performance over time.

Because the lender will be doing these analyses, it would be a good idea for the borrower to be prepared. Here again, a good financial advisor can be very helpful.

✔ **An ESOP as a Highly Leveraged Transaction (HLT)**   In closely held companies, the vast majority of ESOPs are done with an eye towards a "Section 1042 rollover." Briefly, this section of the Internal Revenue Code permits deferral of capital gains on shares sold to a closely held C corporation's ESOP if, after the transaction, the ESOP owns at least 30% of the company and the selling stockholder reinvests the proceeds in "qualified replacement property." This generally means an investment in the stocks or bonds of domestic operating corporations. It could be an investment in a single company or in a diversified portfolio.

If borrowed funds are used to generate the cash that goes "out the door" to the selling stockholder, the increase in debt combined with the decrease in equity may create what used to be called a "highly leveraged transaction" (HLT). Although the term is no longer of legal significance, the concept continues to be important.

A major corporate event such as an acquisition, buyout, or recapitalization that: (1) at least doubles the company's liabilities, resulting in total liabilities being at least 50% of total assets (including intangibles), or (2) results in total liabilities (at least 25% of which are attributable to the event) being more than 75% of total assets (including intangibles), will generally flag a transaction for special attention and higher levels of analysis.

SUGGESTION. Limit the leverage of an ESOP. The first and simplest way to do this is for the current owners of a closely held company to accomplish their transfer of ownership to an ESOP in stages rather than all at once. Only 30% ownership by the ESOP is needed to obtain Section 1042 treatment. The ESOP can borrow to reach this threshold in the first year and increase its position two or three years later as cash flow and credit considerations allow. If the company's existing level of debt means that even the 30% level is too much of a stretch, perhaps 20% or 25% ownership by the ESOP can be debt-financed. Then, just before this stock purchase, the company can contribute newly issued shares to the ESOP so that pro forma for the purchase its total ownership position will exceed the 30% threshold. (This gambit may be limited, however, by Section 415 limits discussed below.)

✔ **Credit Enhancement**   The level of debt needed to achieve the 30% ESOP ownership target required for a Section 1042 rollover may be beyond the level of a bank loan. Or, even if the 30% level is achieved, the sale of a higher percentage may be desired, and this percentage may also be beyond the level of a bank loan.

> *SUGGESTION.* There are two basic approaches that may be taken. The first approach is for the selling owner to take back a deeply subordinated note in exchange for some part of his or her shares. This defers the capital gains only until cash payments of principal are received. At that time, the receipt of the cash is taxable, and the seller cannot elect the Section 1042 tax deferral.
>
> In a variation of this first approach, the seller can obtain the Section 1042 tax deferral by taking other assets (if they are available) and investing them in qualified replacement property. The seller then elects to treat the principal amount of the note to the ESOP as taxable income in the first year (that is, the seller opts out of treating the sale as an installment note for tax purposes) and elects the Section 1042 tax deferral. In that case, tax is due only on the annual interest payments because subsequent principal payments will be characterized as a return on capital.
>
> The second approach is for the selling owner to guarantee the debt of the company (and the ESOP), and to back that guarantee by pledging to the bank the "1042 rollover portfolio" of securities. (The ESOP sale proceeds must be invested in qualified securities to defer capital gains taxes.) The most common way to structure this guarantee is for the selling owner to invest the proceeds in a portfolio of highly rated, nonvolatile securities, such as AA or AAA rated adjustable rate preferred stock or notes. Because of the adjustable rate feature and high rating, the portfolio should maintain its par value and permit the highest possible collateral value. Typically, as a company gradually reduces its debt, these securities would be released from the collateral pool as appropriate. However, it should be noted that while a pledge of collateral may strengthen a borrower's case, it may not overcome all of a lender's concerns.

In both of the above approaches (a subordinated note and a guarantee through a pledge of securities), the selling owner may be retaining significant ongoing risk related to the success of the company. In some cases the selling owner may have both sold ownership and conceded control to other managers, but he or she is still essentially reinvesting in the company when receiving a subordinated note or pledging proceeds back as collateral. The amount of subordinated debt the selling owner will take, or the amount of securities that the selling owner will pledge back, is a function of the degree of risk that the owner is willing to assume. If the selling owner is supporting the transaction through a guarantee in the form of a mechanism such as the above, lenders may request to see his or her past tax returns as part of their due diligence procedures.

ESOP Loan Sizing and Structure

✔ **"Sizing" an ESOP Loan**   As noted above, the size of a loan to finance an ESOP is limited first by the debt capacity of the sponsoring company. Projections of cash flows and balance sheet coverages will have to be prepared demonstrating an ability to repay any loans in the "base case" created by the lender.

The size and structure of both the "outside" (bank) loan and of the "inside" loan from the company to the ESOP will be controlled by certain ESOP law considerations. The key limiting issue is the size of the payroll of the company, because an ESOP is a defined contribution employee benefit plan. In a standard "C" corporation, the combined total of other continuing defined contribution employee benefit plans and the ESOP's tax-deductible principal payments is limited to 25% of "qualifying payroll," but not more than $40,000 per participant (as indexed for inflation). Interest expense is allowed above the 25% limit. (For an S corporation, the 25% limit must cover the total of both principal and interest payments.) There are also limitations relating to contributions allocated to "highly compensated employees" (i.e., 5%-plus owners and other defined employees). The intent of the law is to provide an employee benefit, and there are a variety of special rules that come into play if a plan has become "top heavy," with too high a percentage of ESOP benefits going to highly compensated employees.

In a standard C corporation, dividends paid on stock held by an ESOP are tax deductible. These dividends may also be applied to principal payments in addition to the 25%-of-payroll limits. (However, for an S corporation, dividends paid on ESOP-held stock are not tax deductible.) Dividends, however, must be reasonable. Many ESOP advisors consider "reasonable" to be an annual dividend limited to no more than 12% to 15% of the value of the ESOP stock. Dividends on ESOP-held stock are also limited by the standard state law earnings and profits tests governing the payment of any dividends.

> *SUGGESTION.* Be sure the company has included all continuing plans, such as 401(k) plans, in calculating its ESOP contribution limits.
>
> The relationship between payroll and the size of proposed principal payments should be carefully examined. This is particularly important where principal payments increase in size over time. When doing a sensitivity analysis to examine the effects of reduced sales volume, the possible inability to deduct principal payments when payroll drops proportionately with sales should be examined.
>
> When preferred or common dividends are used in the cash flows to generate tax deductions, examine the "reasonableness" of these dividends.

✔ **Structuring the Loan** An ESOP must be a term loan, and will generally be drawn by (or guaranteed by) the sponsoring company. American Institute of Certified Public Accountants (AICPA) Statement of Position (SOP) 93-6 requires that all ESOP loans be placed directly on the balance sheet of the sponsoring company, even if the loan is not guaranteed by the company.

Traditionally, commercial banks have been providers of senior debt. The typical features of these loans are, roughly:

- A maximum maturity of five to seven years.
- Amortization of principal starting no later than the loan's second year.
- A total size no more than:
  ‣ Approximately three to four times annual cash flow;
  ‣ Approximately 50% to 65% of market value capitalization; or

‣ The orderly liquidation value of available collateral. A typical liquidation "borrowing base" might be equal to 80% of receivables, 60% of book value of inventories, etc., plus an advance against the value of fixed assets.

All of these will be very specific to the individual situation. The exact structure of principal and interest payments on the ESOP loan will be controlled by the size of the maximum tax deductible ESOP contribution that the company can make, given its payroll base.

A leveraged ESOP (or HLT) will often result in more debt than can be provided within traditional bank senior debt limits. Subordinated debt can be added below the senior debt in order to increase the level of total debt provided, and hence to permit the shareholders to sell a larger share of their ownership to the ESOP. Subordinated debt typically is unsecured and has, roughly:

- A maturity of 7 to 12 years.
- No amortization of principal for the first 5 or more years or until the senior debt is repaid.
- A high interest rate, which is sometimes supplemented by an "equity kicker" in the form of warrants, conversion to common stock, etc.

The level of total debt in the transaction that the market will accept has varied over time. For example, lenders in the mid- and late 1980s sometimes allowed the total of senior and subordinated debt to reach as high as 90% of total market value capitalization. This percentage trended down through the 1990s, and in the current environment, lenders expect the total of senior and subordinated debt to be no more than either four and a half to five and a half times annual cash flow, or 70% of the total capitalization.

Sometimes subordinated debt cannot be obtained at a cost that management is willing to accept. Also, the above assumes that "total capitalization" is the same as "market value," generally defined by a "multiple of cash flow" calculation. Lenders and owners can have differing opinions as to appropriate market value.

SUGGESTION. As with the above suggestion for avoiding HLT status, do the deal in stages. Alternatively, be willing to accept the need for substantial equity kickers to obtain subordinated financing, or the selling shareholder can consider pledging back some of his or her proceeds as collateral security for the ESOP loan.

Still another idea would be for the current shareholder(s) to sell a portion of the company to an independent third party, who might provide liquidity to the company or increase the equity base of the company.

Everything else aside, the key consideration in the total debt analysis is the sensitivity cases to the financial projections that are prepared by the lenders. These sensitivity cases will incorporate the results of the lender's due diligence and the risks of the transaction.

✔ **Determining the Borrower of the Loan**   The loan can be either (1) to the ESOP itself or (2) in a structure of parallel "back-to-back" "inside" and "outside" loans from the lender to the company and from the company to the ESOP. There are advantages and disadvantages to each structure. For example, a direct loan to the ESOP can help a U.S. multinational solve a foreign tax credit limitation problem. Alternatively, a back-to-back structure is sometimes perceived as providing extra legal comfort for the lender from a fraudulent conveyance perspective or as an extra shield for the lender from fiduciary concerns.

SUGGESTION. As a general practice, especially in middle-market lending, lenders will usually insist that loans should go first to the company—the direct source of repayment. However, market practice has accepted direct loans to the ESOP in large transactions for Fortune 500 companies.

Cash Flow Effects of an ESOP

✔ **Employee Motivation**   There is a variety of anecdotal and statistical evidence that an ESOP can be a powerful motivational tool when coupled with a company's commitment to employee participation and communication. These ESOP companies do seem to perform better. It is difficult to incorporate "employee enthusiasm and morale" into cash flow projections. However, companies will often project improvement in operating efficiencies. In a close call, a lender might give a little extra credence to these projections when an ESOP is also being put in place. This will be particularly so for service companies and others where retention of employee talent may be critical.

✔ **Interest Rates/Tax-Deductible Principal and Dividend Payments** In a properly structured transaction, the ongoing tax advantages of an ESOP, and in particular, the "effective" deductibility of principal payments, should be a "given" and their loss a highly unlikely event. (Standard documentation of an ESOP loan includes a legal opinion as to the proper formation of the ESOP and its compliance with appropriate regulations.) However, it is possible for a transaction to lose certain advantages through actions or inactions of the sponsoring company. Also, if the cash flow and value of the company declines, its ability to pay "reasonable" (tax-deductible) dividends may decline.

It is also possible that Congress could eliminate one or all of these benefits. (In practice, based on precedents such as the changes to the rules governing Industrial Revenue bonds and the 1989 and 1996 revisions to laws governing ESOPs, it is likely that existing loans would be "grandfathered" in any new legislation—certainly as to the tax deductibility of principal.)

In a leveraged ESOP or other such tightly structured transaction, the adequacy of cash flows for debt repayment may depend on the tax advantages noted above.

> *SUGGESTION.* A sensitivity analysis should be done to understand the effect of these unlikely occurrences on the cash flows. If the maximum level of ESOP contributions is assumed throughout the term of the loan, there should be enough cushion in the ratio of cash flow to debt service to withstand moderate changes in the tax deductibility of ESOP contributions and dividends.

✔ **Repurchase Obligation** The law requires that a closely held company must repurchase distributed shares from employees who have left the company if the employees so wish or if the bylaws of the company restrict stock ownership in a fashion so as to force repurchase.

The repurchases must be made for "fair market value" as

independently determined at least annually by an outside appraiser. (In a publicly traded company, employees can sell shares in the open market to obtain liquidity for their ESOP distributions.)

The annual cash flow effect of the repurchase obligation is a function of the company's age profile and turnover rate. (A high turnover rate will reduce the number of shares vesting and potentially subject to repurchase during the period in question.)

For the initial lender to an ESOP, the company's potential repurchase obligation is generally not a problem. The law generally allows a company to defer its obligation to repurchase shares bought with an ESOP loan until the loan is fully repaid. Most companies make an exception for employees who die or leave the company as they reach "normal retirement age" and repurchase their shares. Repurchase obligations arising from these exceptions are usually not material drains on the company's cash flow. Further cash flow protection can be gained by vesting the employees in their shares no faster than the law allows—either five-year "cliff" vesting or seven-year gradual vesting.

Finally, additional protection can be obtained by having the ESOP documents provide for payment of the repurchase obligation over five years (the maximum the law allows) rather than all in one year. Given all of the above, the repurchase obligation should not be too much of a problem for the initial lender.

> *SUGGESTION.* Lenders will generally inquire about a repurchase obligation study. They will also be sure the ESOP plan document provides for no repurchases other than as required by law until the ESOP loan is retired, for vesting no faster than the law requires, and for the company to have the option to make payment on the repurchase obligation as slowly as the law allows. If the company already has a plan in place that does not contain these protections, lenders will likely request that the plan be amended to incorporate these provisions for all shares purchased with the proceeds of the new loan.

For a subsequent lender to a closely held company with an existing ESOP, these same issues exist. Since here the repurchase obligation cannot be fully deferred until the repayment of the new loan, close study must be made of this off-balance sheet repurchase obligation. Even so, the liability depends on the value of the shares, which in turn depends on the equity value of the company.

On a practical rather than theoretical basis, this means that the repurchase obligation has some self-correcting features. On the one hand, if the company is very successful, the value of the equity, and potential repurchase obligation will go up. But in this situation, it is likely the company has the financial strength to releverage to meet the obligation, or to eliminate the problem by going public. On the other hand, if the company is in financial distress and cannot meet its obligations to its lenders, the value of the equity will be very limited. Therefore, the potential repurchase obligation should be a significantly lower risk when a company is in financial distress.

> *SUGGESTION.* Lenders will examine the company's analysis of its repurchase obligation—preferably an analysis done by an outside, independent firm. They may also request a covenant that the valuation study establishing the price for the repurchase of any shares be done more frequently than once a year, if requested by the bank or if certain financial tests are not met.

For either a public or a closely held company, an additional complication can arise when the ESOP owns an issue of convertible preferred and the company has "guaranteed" the minimum value of the preferred per share. This overrides the comfort of the self-correcting general rule noted above. The size of the potential liability this creates must be examined. A lender's "ESOP horror story" is an ESOP that provides for very quick vesting; guaranteed repurchase at a preset minimum price, rather than at market value if lower; and no delay on satisfaction of the repurchase obligation. When the company runs into trouble, departing employees severely accelerate the cash drain.

> *SUGGESTION.* Lenders will generally be very cautious when an ESOP guarantees a floor price or value on shares for repurchase obligation.

✔ **Diversification Requirement** A precursor of the full repurchase obligation is the diversification requirement, which is applicable to all ESOP companies, both public and closely held. When employees reach age 55, with 10 years of participation in the ESOP, and have allocated to their accounts shares acquired by the ESOP after 1986, then they must be allowed the right to diversify 25% of their ESOP portfolios out of company stock if they so wish. The requirement goes to 50% at age 60.

This requirement cannot be deferred until the loan that purchases the shares is fully repaid. In a closely held company this is a potential cash drain. Nonetheless, for the initial lender this may not be too much of an issue because it is not a factor until 10 years after the ESOP is formed.

> *SUGGESTION.* Lenders will be sure the repurchase obligation study projects the cash flow needed for the diversification requirement; they will check for this potential problem even if a full repurchase study is not done.

✔ **Accounting Issues** The standard method of accounting for ESOPs was originally Financial Accounting Standards Board (FASB) Statement of Position (SOP) 76-3, which places the ESOP debt on the books of the company and offsets the debt with a "contra account" in equity. As the debt is repaid, the contra-equity amount is correspondingly reduced. A more recent pronouncement, AICPA SOP 93-6, continued this position (the ESOP debt is on the books, even if not guaranteed by the sponsor) and added significant detail to the calculations of EPS. The FASB's Emerging Issues Task Force (EITF) is also looking at the issue of the "off balance sheet" repurchase obligation. It is possible that FASB may ultimately decide that the net present value of this should be placed on the balance sheet, in the same manner that unfunded pension liabilities are now on the balance sheet.

If the ESOP holds common stock that does not pay a dividend, the entire amount of the ESOP principal payments will be recorded on the income statement as employee compensation expense. If a dividend is received by the ESOP, a variety of tests are applied to determine the proper accounting treatment.

> *SUGGESTION.* Be aware of the issues involved and be sure that the company is in compliance with AICPA SOP 93-6. Be sure to distinguish between accounting treatment and true cash flows.

Covenants and Documentation

An ESOP loan is documented just like any other loan, with all of the standard covenants, controls, security, etc. There are, however, a number of special quirks.

✔ **Financial Covenants** Any "normal" income statement-related covenants will be distorted by the inclusion of the ESOP debt principal payments (or accruals) as employee compensation expense. Further adjustment will be required for interest income received by the sponsoring company from the ESOP, and when preferred or common dividends are used as a planned source of ESOP debt repayment.

> *SUGGESTION.* Income statement-related covenants such as fixed charge coverages should be properly defined to adjust for the above in order to accurately test cash flow performance.

After-tax cash flow coverage in some appropriate form should be added as a covenant in order to recognize the importance of the tax deductibility of principal and to trigger acceleration if the tax deductibility of principal is lost and therefore cash flow is inadequate. (As previously noted, this is mostly an issue in covenants for leveraged ESOPs.)

✔ **Legal Representations, Warranties, and Indemnities** The "standard" documentation for an ESOP loan may include (1) legal opinions regarding the ESOP's formation, tax status, and the tax status of the ESOP loan; (2) a "fairness" opinion from the ESOP's financial advisor that the transaction meets Department of Labor standards for ESOP purchases of stock (especially significant for a closely held company, where there are multiple equity investors in an LBO, or where a non-traded security such as a convertible preferred is issued); and (3) fraudulent conveyance concerns (especially if the ESOP is part of an LBO).

SUGGESTION. Each lender and lender's counsel will have to prepare positions on these issues. The important item here is to be sure that both the borrower's and lender's internal (or outside) counsel is familiar with the special issues involved in ESOPs.

Conclusion

An ESOP loan is, first and foremost, a loan. The credit decision—cash flow, collateral, character—should stand independent of the special issues of the ESOP. If a company is creditworthy, then the complications of an ESOP loan are manageable. The potential cash flow constraints and advantages of the ESOP rules are relatively straightforward, and extra risks such as repurchase obligation are measurable. An ESOP loan may be a bit more complex than a "straightforward" HLT or LBO, but not unmanageably so. The company and ESOP will often have in addition to the ESOP counsel an independent financial advisor or counsel, who can provide significant input and creativity on the ESOP structuring issues, allowing the lender to focus on the credit issues and financing structure. Finally, the selling shareholder can enhance the credit by providing subordinated debt or guarantees, though this continues the selling shareholder's exposure to the risks of the business.

All that remains is for the borrower to be properly prepared for the loan application. A full set of historical financials, detailed financial projections, knowledge of the company's valuation, a good handle on repurchase obligation issues, a management and succession plan, and an understanding of some of the credit constraints that the lender will operate under are crucial.

ESOP loans can be a "win-win" situation. The selling owner of a closely held C corporation can indefinitely defer capital gains on the sale, the effective tax deductibility of the principal payments can increase the debt capacity of the transaction, and the availability of the rollover portfolio can provide additional collateral support to the transaction beyond that available in a comparable non-ESOP leveraged transaction.

CHAPTER 3

UNDERSTANDING ESOP VALUATION

COREY ROSEN

Why Do You Need a Valuation?

There is a T-shirt in the Exploratorium museum in San Francisco with a picture of Albert Einstein in a policeman's hat. The legend on the T-shirt says "186,000 miles per second. It's not just a good idea, it's the law." If you want to have an ESOP in a closely held company, an independent, outside valuation is not just a good idea, it's the law. You must have an appraiser figure out what a willing buyer would pay a willing seller, assuming both have all the relevant information they need to make the transaction.

Congress created this requirement because of a number of disturbing cases in which ESOPs paid considerably more than what an outside appraiser would have said was fair. The price was set by the company's board or even by the seller to an ESOP. The excessively high price the plan paid may have been great for the seller, but it caused some of these companies to fail. Congress wanted to protect the taxpayer's investment in ESOPs. Absent a required valuation, there could be no assurance that at least some business owners would not use the substantial tax incentives provided under the law more for their own benefit than that of the plan's participants.

The NCEO also publishes this chapter as the booklet *Understanding ESOP Valuation.*

Even if it were not the law, it would be a good idea to have a valuation for several reasons. First, if an owner is selling to an ESOP, a price determined by a formula or by the board, for instance, is almost certainly going to be wrong. Many people call us saying "Why can't we just use book value?" or some other formula. But book value usually understates the real worth of ownership in most businesses, just as most other formulas are misleading. Most businesses are worth some multiple of their earnings, earnings that are generated not just by assets, but by such intangibles as reputation, expertise, contacts, innovative ideas and processes, etc. On the other hand, a minority interest in a company may, in some cases, be worth less than a simple book value calculation may suggest, and some businesses' assets may be worth more than the future earnings they can create in that particular enterprise (real estate may fit this definition, for instance). So if you are selling for book value, you are almost certainly not getting a correct price.

On the other hand, other owners call us and say they know that in their industry, businesses sell for an average of x times earnings or some other multiple. But your business is not likely to be average. If in using a formula you come up with a value that is just a few percentage points higher or lower than a more accurate assessment of your company's value, the costs will be much greater than the cost of a valuation. For instance, if your formula is off 3%, and your value is $2 million, then the formula is either costing you (if it is too low) or the ESOP (if it is too high) $60,000, many times the cost of an independent appraiser.

Second, an independent appraisal is essential to convincing employees that an ESOP is a good thing for them. If they believe that the ESOP is overpaying for its shares—that it is just a clever way, for instance, for the owner to take money out of the company on a tax-preferred basis—then employees are going to be very skeptical about the plan. In fact, before the requirement for an independent appraisal became law in 1984, the U.S. General Accounting Office pointed to a number of cases in which ESOPs had significantly overpaid for their shares, making it difficult or impossible for the company the employees inherited to pay off its loans.

Finally, having an appraisal can be a useful business planning tool. After all, the appraiser's report, which can run to hundreds of pages, is all about comparing your business both to other businesses and to other uses for the money invested in your company. It thus provides a detailed benchmark to determine how you are doing and what elements of your strategy can be changed to improve equity value.

How Often Must an Appraisal Be Performed?

The law requires appraisals to be done at least annually, but there may be circumstances that require a more frequent appraisal. The law also requires that ESOP transactions be conducted at the current fair market value. That means that any time the ESOP buys or sells stock, it should, in theory, be based on a fair market valuation as of the date of the transaction.

If the ESOP is buying shares from an owner or the company, for instance, it should try to time its purchase to coincide with the most recent appraisal as closely as possible. The IRS prefers that the transaction be accompanied by a valuation opinion letter stating that the valuation is effective as of that date. On an ongoing basis, all transactions related to plan distributions (such as a departing employee selling shares back to the company or the plan) should normally occur at a specific annual date that will be timed as closely as possible with the annual appraisal. In practice, what this usually means is that the appraiser provides a report on a regular schedule and the plan administrator closes the plan year as soon as possible after that. Statements are then mailed to employees, and transactions are completed during a short window following the closing.

But what happens if there is an ESOP transaction that is not in this window? Just how close is close enough? Unfortunately, there is no useful guidance on this. Say, for instance, that an appraisal is completed as of April 1 ("as of" here means that the price set in the report is effective that date, not that the report is completed that date). On July 1, the ESOP buys shares from an owner, or an employee sells stock back to the ESOP. Is the April 1 appraisal acceptable? The only answer is that the trustee of the ESOP—the person or persons who make decisions for the plan—must be able to show that there is no reason to believe that there will be any significant change in value over that time, either from internal factors (a change in the company's revenues, costs, assets, or other issues that affect value) or external factors (the market for equities has changed, such as a sharp drop in the S&P index or a hike in interest rates). Absent the ability to say that confidently, a new appraisal is needed. Your ESOP advisors should be looked to for guidance on these issues any time there is any doubt.

Who Performs an Appraisal?

The law requires an independent, outside appraisal from someone who is customarily in the business of doing business appraisals. There has never been a precise definition of what "independent" is, however. Clearly, some people are excluded—your board, your attorney, your brother-in-law, your CFO, your CPA, or anyone else with a direct financial relationship with the company. But what about your CPA firm (but not the person doing your books), or the valuation advisor who is affiliated with your attorney? Many people argue that if your CPA firm is large and can establish a "firewall" separating its audit and valuation sections, then that is acceptable. Others contend that even this is risky. Similarly, some people say you can use firms affiliated with your advisers (such as a valuation firm that pays a fee to your attorney for referrals), but most experts would argue that is not a wise policy.

We at the NCEO strongly suggest that you pick a firm that has no other business relationship with your company than the appraisal itself. Almost all the lawsuits involving ESOPs concern valuation. The law looks primarily to process, not results, in determining whether the appraisal was fair to the ESOP. An appraisal done by a truly independent, qualified firm establishes a degree of credibility not possible any other way. With any other firm, there is always the possibility that the appraisal was done with an eye toward getting or keeping the company's business for the other parts of the firm or the affiliated parties involved in other parts of the transaction. The costs will rarely be lower in using someone not truly independent, so it is best to err on the side of caution.

The other major issue in determining whether an appraiser is qualified is competence. Here there are two areas to evaluate. The first is general business appraisal competence. Anyone can be a business appraiser. No specific degree and no licensing procedure is required by states or other entities. The appraisal industry does try to be self-regulating, however.

There are a number of organizations, offering a wide variety of designations, that provide some kind of business appraisal certification. Among these are the American Society of Appraisers (ASA), the National Association of Certified Valuation Analysts (NACVA), the Institute of Business Appraisers (IBA), and the American Institute of Certified Public Accountants (AICPA). Each organization provides some kind of technical education program providing certification designations. There are so many designations now that they can become quite confusing. It is worth asking an appraiser what designations he or she has and what was required to obtain them, but making comparisons on designations alone may be difficult.

In addition to these qualifications, you should also look at experience, in-house training requirements for the firm, whether the appraiser has spoken or published on the subject, and, of course, references.

Business appraisal competence is not enough, however. As will become clear later, there are many ESOP-specific issues. These issues can have a dramatic impact on the final valuation. Your appraiser should be able to demonstrate specific experience and expertise in ESOPs. Ask for a list of ESOP clients and call them. Find out whether the appraiser belongs to at least one of the relevant professional organizations (the NCEO and the ESOP Association); subscribes to the only professional journal in the field, *The Journal of Employee Ownership Law and Finance;* regularly attends professional conferences on the subject; and has spoken or written on ESOP-specific issues. If the appraiser claims to have ESOP expertise but does not meet these criteria, look elsewhere.

How Do You Find a Good Appraiser?

Both the NCEO and the ESOP Association maintain lists of appraisers and other ESOP professionals that are available to members. Neither group endorses the people listed in the guides, but at least this provides assurance that the appraisers are involved in the relevant professional organizations. Most active ESOP appraisers will appear on both lists. Your other professional advisors usually will also have recommendations, and you should ask other ESOP companies whom they have used.

One issue to decide is whether to pick an appraiser from a large or small firm. Large firms typically have an appraisal reviewed by one or more other staff members and may have additional credibility should there be a legal challenge. Some small firms, however, have excellent reputations and also may provide for internal reviews. Generally, large firms charge more, but this is not always the case. While there is not a right or wrong answer here, size per se is probably not a critical issue when comparing firms of comparable price, competence, and compatibility.

In picking an appraiser, it is wise to interview at least two or three candidates. You will find that there are significant variations in price, experience, and appraisal philosophy. The first two are obvious things to look for, but the third may seem a little confusing. Why ask about philosophy?

Different ESOP appraisers have different approaches to key appraisal issues, such as discounts for lack of control or liquidity (these are discussed below), or in their general appraisal approach (such as whether they rely more on earnings multiples or on comparable companies). These will have a potentially dramatic affect on value. Initial assumptions tend to get locked into your ongoing ESOP appraisal. It will always arouse suspicion if, a few years after the first ESOP appraisal, you decide you are unhappy with the approach and choose someone else who comes in with a different set of assumptions. Your business won't have changed, but ESOP participants and the IRS may now see a very different appraisal number. At best, you have a serious communications problem; at worst, you have a lawsuit or problem with the government.

Similarly, it is both expensive and risky to decide after the initial appraisal that you do not like the result and ask to have a second appraisal from someone else. The appearance, at least, is that you are shopping for an appraisal advantageous to you, not accepting an objective report. To head off such complications, the ESOP trustee or the person who will become the trustee (as we shall see, the appraiser works for the trustee) should interview appraisers beforehand.

Some appraisers, as well as some legal advisors, may tell you that this too makes it appear you are shopping the appraisal. But we would argue, along with most of the ESOP legal community, that without these discussions the trustee cannot make an informed decision on who is best to do the appraisal.

Now, however, comes the tricky part. These interviews must be designed to find out what approaches are going to be in the best long-term interest of the ESOP and its participants. The goal is not to find the appraiser who will come up with the highest price. Instead, the trustee should be looking to assure, as best as possible, that the appraisal will support the long-term viability of the plan and that the appraisal will use methodologies that are generally accepted by the appraisal community and the regulatory authorities. That means the price will not be so high as to endanger the company's ability to pay for it nor so low that the current sellers will not want to sell. The appraisal assumptions and procedures must also assure that future participant distributions will be at their proper value. The ultimate price must fit within the range of what reasonable appraisers could agree is not more than fair market value.

Admittedly, these are somewhat vague guidelines, but ESOP appraisal is an art, not a science. While the process cannot be exact, however, it can and must be informed. A careful discussion with the appraiser about these issues prior to engagement can avoid confusion and unhappiness down the line. Note, however, that the appraiser may (appropriately) say that an initial discussion does not provide enough information to make an assessment of which approaches will work best.

Who Hires the Appraiser?

The appraiser's client, by law, is the ESOP trust, no matter who actually writes the checks to cover the fees. This has important implications. First, the letter of engagement should clearly specify that the appraiser is working for the ESOP. Second, it means the appraiser is not trying to find the highest price that can be justified or, as in some tax-oriented appraisals, the lowest. Third, it should remind everyone involved that the point of the appraisal is to protect the interests of the ESOP participants from paying more than fair market value.

Is the Appraised Price the One the ESOP Pays?

Once the appraiser has provided a report stating what the fair market value is, that is not the end of the story. Many people incorrectly assume that the fair market value given in the appraiser's report is the price that the ESOP must pay. Instead, the law requires that the ESOP cannot pay *more* than fair market value. Indeed, it is the responsibility of the ESOP trustee to negotiate the best price possible.

This negotiation might take a number of tacks. In a few cases, the seller prefers to sell for a lower price, usually because of concerns about the ability of the ESOP to repay the loan or just because the owner wants to be generous. In others, the trustee argues that tax benefits to a seller to an ESOP should come partly back to the ESOP in the form of a lower price. It is the ESOP, after all, that justifies the lower price as a result of its tax advantages. In still other cases, the ESOP trustee is simply bargaining for a better deal and, given the lack of other options the seller may have, is able to exert some leverage. Finally, some owners are simply willing to offer a lower price to make the buyout easier for the company to afford.

These scenarios all envision using an ESOP to buy shares from an existing owner. Sometimes an ESOP acquires new shares, such as when it borrows money to purchase shares to help finance growth, or when it accepts contributions of shares. In these cases, the trustee has less negotiating leverage because the contributions to the ESOP are diluting other owners, not buying their shares. Still, the size of a loan might be such that a lower price is needed to fit within legal requirements, or owners may wish to add another bargain element for the ESOP.

Theoretically, a sale at a price far below fair market value could trigger a gift tax for the ESOP (which would then pay unrelated business income tax). In practice, we have never seen this become an issue. There is enough leeway in how shares are valued so that by varying assumptions this problem can almost always be overcome.

What Does the Appraiser Need from You?

In preparing an appraisal report, the appraiser will need a lot of data from you. The more precise and well prepared these data are, the better (and possibly cheaper) the appraisal will be. The following list indicates the key items appraisers generally need, although there may be other things requested:

- Financial statements, typically for the last five to ten years, preferably audited (but many smaller companies will present only reviewed statements). Income statements, balance sheets, cash flow and capital statements, and any explanatory footnotes or other material are included.

- Budgets or projections

- List of subsidiaries, if any

- Leases and contracts

- Compensation schedules

- Prior appraisals

- Dividend history and expectations

- Legal documents

- Prior sales or offers

- Shareholder list

- ESOP documents

- Operational information, such as sales by customer, patents, departmental budgets, competitors, etc.

In addition to a review of these documents, the appraiser will want to interview management and possibly board members, suppliers, customers, advisors, or anyone else deemed to have critical information. One or more site visits will be arranged. During these interviews, any significant issues that could materially affect operations, such as a pending environmental liability, a new competitor, management changes, or a patent expiration, for instance, should be thoroughly discussed.

What Is in the Appraisal Report?

Valuation reports can run from several pages to hundreds of pages, depending on the complexity of the company and the terms of the engagement. The report will cover several issues. The basis for the appraisal of the company as an enterprise should be thoroughly explained and justified (for instance, if the appraiser chose to use an earnings ratio as a key element, why that was more appropriate in this case than some other methodology). Then there should be a discussion of any discounts or premiums applied to that value for the shares the ESOP is purchasing. Again, a thorough explanation of assumptions and rationale should appear. The data used for making the determination should be outlined, and any weightings or judgments used in assessing these data should be elaborated. Any special factors that affect valuation findings, such as a change in management that could reduce future value, should be covered. Reports usually also include a number of charts and tables showing different indications of value based on different methods.

In addition to these matters, the report should follow the guidelines included in the Department of Labor's proposed regulations concerning valuation. Among other things, these include a discussion of the business, its markets, and general economic considerations affecting value. The company's book value should be considered, along with any goodwill or other intangible assets and the company's dividend-paying history and capacity. The price of similar companies, if any, should be provided. Finally, issues relating to marketability and control concerns need to be reviewed.

The final valuation will be a blending of these issues. Because there is no formula for valuations, however, each report will be different.

Steps in the Valuation Process: What Is Fair Market Value and How Is It Calculated?

In calculating how much the ESOP can pay, the first step is to determine how much the business is worth as an entity. There are three basic approaches used to determine this: the asset approach, the market approach, and the income approach.

✔ **Asset Approach** This is the simplest approach and one many closely held companies already use to value their shares for purchases by key employees. It is also the least used method in ESOP appraisals. In this approach, a company is assessed based on either the liquidation value of its assets or its adjusted book value. The adjusted net asset methodology approach takes the balance sheet and transforms it from an accounting document to an economic one. For instance, an asset may be fully depreciated on the balance sheet, but still have resale value on the market. Liabilities may not appear on the balance sheet because they are contingent, such as a possible environmental issue (cleaning up a landfill, for instance). Inventories also need to be adjusted for what they could currently sell for in the market. Any accounts receivable and payable not on the balance sheet need to be considered. Any intangible, but marketable, assets (such as a trade name) need to be assessed.

While these methods are simple, they are also usually wrong. People usually want to buy a business because it can yield them a return on their investment; the ESOP always looks at a purchase this way. While a company's assets are part of what creates an income stream in a company, they are only part of it. All sorts of other factors—expertise, reputation, contacts, processes, labor practices, and other issues—condition how much a company can make. The asset approach has even less relevance when only a minority stake is being sold because minority owners cannot force a liquidation of assets.

✔ **Market Approach** The next approach is to see what, if any, evidence there is of how much people would pay for stock in the company or comparable companies. There may be, for instance, a history of stock sales in the company, or there could be other valid offers. These offers, however, do not necessarily establish a value that the ESOP can pay.

First, the offers may have been for control when the ESOP is not buying control (or vice-versa). Stock is worth more when it is part of a control purchase, as discussed more fully below. Second, the offer may have come from another company with a synergistic interest in the target company. If International MegaCompany can gain operating efficiencies, or eliminate competition, by buying Pete's Pizza Parlors, they will pay more for Pete's than would a buyer who could not capture these efficiencies. The ESOP is always a *financial* buyer; it must be able to justify its purchase based on the return that investment yields as a stand-alone company, although heavy acquisition activity in a given industry may influence market pricing upward and should be considered. Third, the offer or sale may have been for less than market value, as often is the case with sales to managers based on book value. These and similar concerns make this methodology useful in providing benchmarks, but far from determinative.

A related methodology is to look at comparable companies. The ideal comparison is another closely held company in the same industry with similar financials. But these ideal companies are hard to find, and, even if found, there are usually no data of any kind on transactions, much less the detailed data to allow apples-to-apples comparisons (such as whether the sale was to a synergistic buyer). Private companies do not have to report such data to any public source, but some valuation companies have access to databases that track sales that their firm has followed.

Better data are available from public companies, but here

several complicating issues arise. First, many public companies have multiple lines of business. Second, they are almost always larger, and often much larger, than the company being appraised. Third, they may have very different capital structures than closely held companies. These and other differences make direct comparisons difficult. Most business appraisers are experienced in dealing with these complications, however, so the data on stock prices in these companies can yield useful insights about the typical ratios (such as share price to annual earnings) that can be applied, with appropriate adjustments, to provide benchmarks for applying multiples to the company being valued. When using public companies, the indicated value for the company being appraised is a minority interest, freely marketable value because the share prices of the publicly traded companies represent small minority interests in the public company.

Another source of market data is comparable companies (including closely held companies) that have been merged and/or acquired. Multiples paid in such comparable transactions are generally applied, with appropriate adjustments, to the subject company's earnings and cash flow. Because the multiples based on these data are calculated using prices paid for entire companies, the indicated value for the subject company is a value for the entire company (enterprise or control value). It may or may not indicate a "liquid" value, depending on whether or not the comparable merged and/or acquired companies were public or privately held at the time of acquisition.

However a market approach is constructed, a company's earnings will be "normalized" to reflect how another buyer would operate the business. This is discussed in more detail below in the section on the income approach to valuation.

✔ **Income Approach** A third set of methodologies falls under the income approach. The basic theory behind these methodologies is that a buyer is looking to make a reasonable return on an investment over an acceptable period of time, given the relative risk of the investment. A theoretical willing buyer is looking at a variety of investment choices. There are safe ones with low returns (CDs, T-bills, etc.), somewhat riskier ones with higher returns (stocks and bonds), and still riskier ones with the highest returns (individual companies). It has to be this way: the higher the risk, the greater the return an investor will demand. In buying a company, then, the investor needs to know two basic things: what the risk is and what the income flow is that will result from the investment. There are a number of ways to conceptualize these factors, but the two most common are referred to as capitalization of free cash flow and discounted cash flow.

Capitalization of Free Cash Flow Method With the capitalization of free cash flow (FCF) method, the appraiser develops an estimate of the company's sustainable level of free cash flow. This is usually based on history and estimates of what future FCF will be. FCF is defined as follows:

> Net Income
> + Non-cash charges (such as depreciation)
> − Increases in working capital
> + Additions to long-term debt
> − Payments of long-term debt
> − Capital expenditures
> = **Free cash flow (FCF)**

Free cash flow is normally used because that is the basis from which an investor can earn a return from the investment either in the form of dividends or investment of the FCF back into the business for future growth. However, some appraisers prefer other variations on the future income theme, such as earnings before interest, taxes, and depreciation.

After these numbers are determined, they are adjusted to reflect nonrecurring items and special considerations. For instance, there may have been a large one-time expense that lowered earnings (and thus FCF) in a prior year, or an anticipated one-time expense in the future projections. Very commonly the pay and perquisites of executives or other employees needs to be adjusted to reflect what the market rates for these individuals are, unless these practices will remain in place after the transaction. If the CEO is making

$400,000 a year and has a company-paid vacation to France every year, the appraiser might determine that these expenses would be substantially reduced if someone else bought the company. This excess is added back to earnings if the levels of compensation will not continue into the future. Similar adjustments to earnings and cash flow are typically made before applying multiples in the market approaches as well. After analyzing historical and potential earnings, the appraiser will determine a single figure called "representative earnings."

Finally, a capitalization rate is applied to these representative cash flows. The concept here involves some complex math, but the basic idea is simple. The appraiser is trying to determine what the present value of a future stream of sustainable FCF is. The rate is derived by subtracting the expected long-run rate of FCF growth from the company's discount rate. The discount rate, in turn, reflects the rate of available risk-free investments and the risk adjustments appropriate for the fact that this is an equity investment made in a company of a certain size (there is less risk in a large company) with specific risk concerns.

For instance, an appraiser might determine that in a particular business, the expected FCF growth rate is 6% per year. The discount rate is 25%. The capitalization rate is now 19%, and this is divided into expected FCF to determine the company's value. If the next year's (or sustainable) FCF is $3 million, the company would be worth $3 million divided by .19, or $15.8 million before considering appropriate discounts or premiums. The underlying concept here is that the investor is looking to obtain a return on investment that justifies the risk. In this case, the return would be 19% on the expected annual FCF.

Discounted Cash Flow Approach   A similar approach is the discounted cash flow method. Here the discount rate (25% in this case) is applied to a measure of FCF. Theoretically, all the earnings could be paid out this way to justify the investment, and this would provide a benchmark for determining value. Again, annualized free cash flows are determined; these are then discounted back to the present at the required rate of return or discount rate. The appraiser will add a terminal value at the end of the forecast period to complete the analysis.

In both methods, attention must be paid to the special tax benefits the ESOP provides the company as these can change expected earnings and cash flow.

What Discounts or Premiums Apply to ESOP Value?

Whether or not any discounts and/or premiums apply to the indicated values derived using the valuation methods described above depends on numerous factors. In ESOP valuations, discounts generally fall into two categories: liquidity and control. These are discussed in more detail below. But before knowing whether to apply a discount, it first must be determined whether or not the valuation is being conducted on a controlling interest (or enterprise) basis or a minority interest basis. Then, depending on the method and data used within the valuation method, appropriate discounts and/or premiums are applied. Similarly, whether to apply a liquidity discount depends on whether the comparisons used to determine value are based on liquid or illiquid interests in companies.

By way of example, assume that the valuation assignment is to determine the enterprise (controlling interest) value of a company and that the appraiser has used market approaches and an income approach. In the market approach, the appraiser used two subsets of information, comparable publicly traded companies and comparable companies that had been merged and/or acquired.

As noted earlier, the value indicated based on comparable publicly traded companies is a minority interest, freely traded (or completely liquid) value. Therefore, in order to arrive at a value for an entire enterprise, it would generally be appropriate to apply a premium for control and a discount for lack of marketability. Conversely, if the valuation assignment were to value the company on a minority interest basis, it would not be appropriate to apply a minority interest discount to the comparable publicly traded approach, because the value indicated already reflects a minority interest discount. It would, however, be appropriate to consider a discount for lack of marketability.

The value indicated from the comparable merged and/or acquired company approach represents an indication of control or enterprise value. Thus, if the subject company is being appraised on a controlling interest basis, then it is not appropriate to apply a control premium to this approach. That would be a double discount because the value is already reflective of controlling interest value since the multiples used in this approach are based on prices paid for entire companies. On the other hand, if the subject company is being valued on a minority interest basis, then it would be appropriate to apply a minority interest discount to this approach. Whether or not a discount for lack of marketability is appropriate using this approach generally depends on if the comparable merged or acquired companies were public at the time of the acquisitions.

The income approach may indicate either a control or minority interest value. Generally speaking, if control level free cash flows were used, the income approach indicates a control value. If minority interest level free cash flows were used, the income approach generally indicates a minority interest value. However, variations in the discount rate and/or free cash flows used may result in some sort of blended indication of value, the subject of which is beyond the scope of this chapter.

The critical element to understand with regard to whether or not discounts and/or premiums are appropriate is that it *depends on the base from which the premiums and/or discounts are proposed.* If discounts are needed, they generally fall into two categories below: liquidity and control.

Liquidity (Marketability) Discounts

If you buy shares in IBM, you can sell them any time and get your money in three days. If you buy stock in Sally's Computers, there is no ready market for the shares. You might not be able to sell them for years, and you may have to settle for less than market price if you need the money and no one is eager to buy. This lack of marketability creates a discount over the price for the sale of otherwise comparable shares in a public company or shares in a closely held company about to be sold (because in this case there is immediate liquidity). So in any closely held company selling shares other than in a total sale, there is a discount over what the price would be for publicly traded shares, usually in the range of 20% to 40% depending on the circumstances, such as any restrictions on the sale of stock, buy-sell agreements, prospects of an initial public offering, dividends, or the availability of other buyers.

Many ESOP appraisers contend that the presence of the ESOP mitigates or even eliminates this discount. ESOP rules require that departing employees have the right to put their shares back to the company (or have the company fund the ESOP to do this) at fair market value. This seems to eliminate the lack of marketability.

The reality is more complicated, however. First, there must be some assurance that the company can really muster the cash to repurchase the shares. Second, the put option does not belong to the ESOP, for whom the appraisal is being made, but the participants in the plan. Third, the put option applies only in a limited window of time and only when people leave the company or can diversify their accounts. That is hardly the equivalent to owning shares in a public company.

Appraisers argue back and forth on the legal and practical issues involved here. The typical discount for lack of marketability in an ESOP company, according to NCEO studies, is 10% to 20%. A higher discount may discourage the seller from selling; one that is too low saddles the ESOP with an obligation on an ongoing basis to buy shares at a price that reflects an aggressive assumption about value (because these assumptions normally have to be carried forward).

Lack of Control (Minority Interest) Discounts and Control Premiums

The second major issue is control. When someone buys a controlling interest in a company, a premium is paid. This is why share values soar in takeover battles. If the ESOP is buying less than control, it pays less per share (a "minority interest") than would a buyer of controlling interest. Studies of control premiums in public company transactions are compiled every year. These typically are in the 30% range, but can vary widely. Again, however, note that it is only appropriate to apply a minority interest discount to a value indication that represents control.

The first source of variation in control premiums is the company's specific situation. In some companies, a 33% stake may carry some limited control rights; in others, even a 51% stake may not convey full control rights. There might be specific shareholder agreements that limit control of any owner, such as a buy-sell agreement, covenants with banks, or contractual obligations. These and other issues make control a more complex concept than "control" or "no control"; there are shadings in between as well.

A second source of variation is what the ESOP will buy in the future. If the ESOP starts at a minority stake but has a right to buy enough to get control in the future, can it pay a control price? Is the seller obliged to sell to the ESOP? Many advisors say yes, provided that the option allows the purchase in not more than three to five years and gives the ESOP trustee control rights even before gaining a numerical controlling interest. Some appraisers take a tougher view, some a more liberal one. Some appraisers even argue that if the ESOP is buying less than 51% in any purchase, it pays a non-control price (for instance, if the ESOP owns 51% and buys another 20%, it would pay a non-control price for this 20%). There are no right or wrong answers, although in all things related to valuation, we would urge a cautious approach.

Note, however, that the decision on whether to pay a control price is not one the appraiser makes. It is the trustee's decision. The appraiser can provide advice on this issue, but the trustee must decide whether the ESOP really has the attributes and rights necessary to allow a control price to be paid.

The Impact of Leverage on Valuation

If the ESOP borrows money, it will have an impact on valuation. The interest expense on the new debt the company now has taken on to fund the ESOP will show up on the balance sheet and, in any event, represents a significant non-productive expense. While this generally will not reduce value dollar-for-dollar (there are ESOP tax benefits, the company may grow, and there is a discount for the future value of money), it will reduce the post-transaction value. This effect will disappear as the loan is repaid.

This impact is important for two reasons. First, employees need to understand why this drop occurs. Their own account values start at the lower value and thus are not reduced by the debt (unless the loan is to a previously existing plan), but they need to understand the issue to avoid communications problems. Other owners will also see their share price drop, of course. If they plan to sell before the ESOP loan is repaid, this could present a problem. In some cases, companies arrange for pro-rata sales from owners to avoid this issue.

Advanced Issues

Valuation is obviously a complex subject. This chapter is only a basic introduction and cannot go into some of the more advanced scenarios that come up in ESOP appraisals. Two, however, deserve brief attention.

One is where an S corporation sets up an ESOP. Under current (2000) law, when the ESOP trustee receives a statement of the pro-rata share of earnings on which it is supposed to pay tax each year, the trustee can ignore it. ESOPs do not have to pay tax on their share of the S corporation's earnings. Whether this should affect the valuation of the company is a subject of dispute, although a developing consensus seems to suggest that S status alone should not affect value in most cases. Clearly, S status with an ESOP can enhance earnings, yet, just as clearly, a potential willing buyer would be unlikely to maintain the ESOP. So from that buyer's standpoint, the future earnings would be unaffected by this special tax benefit. No standard practices have yet developed on this issue, so ESOP trustees should discuss the subject with their advisors carefully before making a decision to switch from C to S status. Similarly, S corporation owners should understand how their appraiser will look at these issues before setting up a plan.

A second issue occurs when there are multiple investors in a transaction with the ESOP. For instance, if the ESOP buys 30% of a company with debt to be paid out of future corporate earnings, while other investors put in hard cash to buy the remaining 70%, should both parties get a dollar-for-dollar allocation? The Department of Labor seems to think so, but ESOP appraisers have developed techniques for using stock with different attributes to allocate equity in a more realistic manner. If your company is this situation, it is vital to review allocation policy closely with advisors.

Conclusion

The requirement to have an ESOP appraisal is designed to assure that the ESOP process is fair to all parties involved. While many business owners would prefer to set their own prices using a formula or a number derived from prior offers, these simplistic approaches rarely result in the price the ESOP would pay as a financial buyer. ESOP trustees, as well as owners, managers, and employees of ESOP companies, need to understand the valuation process well.

CHAPTER 4

ESOP FEASIBILITY

RONALD J. GILBERT
JOSEPH V. RAFFERTY

Whenever the subject of ESOP feasibility is discussed, certain basics will always or *should* always be examined:

- Is the valuation acceptable to the selling shareholder(s) and to the ESOP trustee or ESOP committee?

- Will the cash flow of the company support the necessary debt to acquire the block of stock being offered to the ESOP?

- Can the divergent interests of various shareholders be accommodated through the ESOP?

- Will the repurchase obligation costs associated with the buyback of stock from departing ESOP participants in a closely held company be manageable?

- At what level of ESOP ownership are current shareholders comfortable?

- Will the required vote pass-through issues in a private company ESOP, and other corporate governance issues, be acceptable to current controlling shareholders?

- Will the required ESOP contributions fall within the allowed limitations?

The authors gratefully acknowledge the assistance of Ronald L. Ludwig in the preparation of this chapter.

In addition to these "standard" items, however, we recommend that a number of other factors be examined in a preliminary assessment to make certain that there are no "red flags" indicating that an ESOP is not feasible or that a better option exists.

Code Section 1042 "Tax-Free" Rollover Tax Benefit and Eligibility

✔ **Tax Benefit**   The major benefit for an eligible shareholder selling stock to an ESOP sponsored by a closely held C corporation is the "tax-free" rollover under Section 1042 of the Internal Revenue Code (the "Code"). However, a significant tax benefit is derived only if there is a substantial difference between the basis in the selling shareholder's stock and the selling price to the ESOP. Most shareholders in closely held companies have a low basis in their stock, and thus most of the selling price of their stock is subject to capital gains taxes. The ability to defer this tax by a sale to the ESOP is thus very attractive. With the current long-term capital gains rate of 15%, and assuming a state capital gains rate of 5%, this tax benefit is worth approximately 20% of the selling price, or $200,000 for every million dollars of the ESOP transaction.

However, to the extent that the stock being sold to the ESOP has a basis that is equal to or greater than the selling price, there is no capital gains tax liability. If the basis is only slightly below the selling price, then the amount of capital gains tax would be minimal. Thus the first item on our "preliminary assessment" or "pre-feasibility" checklist is the basis of stock versus the selling price.

An example of shares that frequently have a basis near the current fair market value of the stock is stock acquired through the distribution from an estate of a deceased shareholder. Thus, children who have recently received stock from the estate of one or both of their parents typically enjoy little or no tax benefit from selling that stock to an ESOP.

✔ **Eligibility**   Stock with a holding period of less than three years, stock acquired in a certain manner, stock of publicly traded companies, S corporation stock, and certain other types of stock are not currently eligible for tax-free rollover treatment.

- Stock acquired in connection with employment is generally not eligible for tax-free rollover treatment. An example would be stock purchased by an employee through a corporate-sponsored stock option program. Stock distributed from a retirement plan, such as a 401(k) plan or an ESOP, also is ineligible for tax-free rollover treatment.

- If the corporation is publicly traded, then it is ineligible for tax-free rollover treatment. This includes stock listed on the New York Exchange, AMEX, or NASDAQ. Even being listed on an electronic exchange may make the shares ineligible for tax-free rollover treatment. The corporation is also an ineligible shareholder for the tax-free rollover.

- Only voting common stock or convertible preferred that is convertible into voting common stock is eligible to be sold for tax-free rollover treatment.

If however, a shareholder holds stock that is ineligible for "tax-free" rollover treatment, it may be possible to have a tax-free recapitalization that converts the existing ineligible stock (nonvoting common, straight preferred, etc.) into eligible stock. The details that determine whether such a recapitalization can be accomplished on a tax-free basis go beyond the scope of this chapter. However, shareholder approval of such recapitalization is normally required. If such a tax-free recapitalization can be accomplished, the holding period of the old security prior to conversion is "tacked on" and can be used to satisfy the three-year holding period required for tax-free rollover treatment. It is not necessary to start the "holding period" clock over again after a conversion.

If the selling shareholder is eligible for "tax-free" rollover treatment, elects this treatment, and the sponsoring company consents to the treatment, then certain shareholders are prohibited from receiving ESOP allocations on any stock subject to the tax-free rollover election. This group of stockholders includes selling shareholders, immediate family members, and any 25%-or-greater shareholder. There is a one-year "look back" in determining these percentages. Furthermore, attribution rules apply. For example, the son of a shareholder owning 75% of the company's stock is deemed to own 75% of the company stock by attribution, and thus is ineligible to receive ESOP allocations on stock sold to the ESOP subject to the tax-free rollover election. There is an exception that allows family members to receive ESOP allocations, but the exception does not apply to the attribution rules, so in most cases family members end up being excluded completely from receiving ESOP allocations.

In smaller companies, especially those with a heavy concentration of family member employees, this allocation prohibition may be a reason for selling shareholders to pay capital gains tax on the sale to the ESOP. Sellers and family members then can receive allocations of stock in the ESOP, and the ESOP allocations will "make up" for some of the capital gains tax that was paid. Without the participation of family members, the covered payroll eligible to receive allocations may be reduced to such a low level that it is not possible to make the necessary contributions to repay ESOP debt without substantially exceeding the ESOP contribution limits.

In larger companies, the exclusion of certain shareholders from ESOP allocations is normally not a problem. To the extent that the corporation wishes to make these excluded shareholders whole, it can do so through some type of nonqualified deferred compensation agreement. This agreement can provide the excluded employee with a future benefit equal in value to the benefit that would have been allocated under the ESOP.

Post-Transaction Decrease in Value

Another issue to be addressed with a leveraged ESOP is the so-called "post-deal drop" in value. In many ESOP transactions the per-share value of the stock will decline after the leveraged ESOP transaction is completed. ESOP appraisers recognize the fact that the corporation now has additional debt and the requirement to service this debt, which may mean decreased net earnings after the ESOP loan is in place. This post-deal drop in value is recovered as ESOP debt is repaid. Thus, its biggest impact will be in the years immediately following the leveraged ESOP transaction.

Alternative Sales Strategies

Even if an individual shareholder owns stock with a low basis relative to the purchase price, and the stock is eligible for tax-free rollover treatment, alternative strategies still may be more attractive from a financial viewpoint.

✔ **Sale to a Strategic or Financial Buyer**   Any sale to an outside buyer is subject to capital gains tax, unless the selling shareholder does a tax-free stock swap, i.e., the shares owned by the selling shareholder are exchanged for stock in the acquiring company. If the price is attractive and the seller feels that the stock of the acquiring company will appreciate in value, then this becomes another way to sell stock on a "tax-free" basis. If the tax-free stock swap is not attractive or available to the selling shareholder, then the strategic buyer would have to pay 25% more than "fair market value" as determined for ESOP purposes if the seller is to net the same amount of proceeds after tax, assuming a 20% combined tax rate. (For example, assume the company's fair market value for ESOP purposes is $1 million and that the seller would receive $1 million on a tax-deferred basis in an ESOP transaction where Section 1042 treatment was elected. Without an ESOP or a tax-free stock swap, the seller would need to be paid $1.25 million to end up with $1 million after being taxed at 20%.) In some instances the strategic or financial buyer will be delighted to pay a 25% or greater premium because of the right "fit" of the acquired company. There can be numerous reasons for this premium, but if the only objective of a selling shareholder is to maximize price, then the sale to a strategic buyer should be explored.

✔ **Initial Public Offering (IPO)**   For some closely held companies, an IPO is another option to be explored. However, even if the company is large enough to consider an IPO, and the company's industry and track record make it a candidate, an IPO will usually not provide shareholders with a significant amount of immediate liquidity. This is due to the fact that investors like to see an IPO where most or all of the proceeds remain in the corporation to be used for business expansion, acquisitions, etc. While the sale of a small amount of individually held stock in an IPO is generally acceptable, the larger percentages usually seen in an ESOP transaction (30% to 100%) would usually be unacceptable in an IPO. It is also not unusual for the stock held by principal shareholders in an IPO to be subject to a "lockup" provision. Such a lockup provision would typically prevent shareholders from selling their stock for a specified period of time, such as one or two years, in the public market. Additionally, since the principal's stock has not been registered, its sale after the lockup is usually restricted under Rule 144.

If, however, the major shareholders are willing to liquidate their holdings over a long period of time and feel that an IPO might provide a premium price for the stock of the company, then it should be considered. Individuals who do sell their stock in the public market will be subject to capital gains taxes in effect at the time the transaction occurs.

The substantial one-time costs of an IPO, even if unsuccessful, plus the annual cost of compliance as a public company, which can approach $1,000,000 per year, even for smaller companies, must be considered.

Financing

Assuming that we have a green light concerning the "tax-free" rollover, or the alternative of paying capital gains tax, and that alternative sales strategies are either unavailable or not in keeping with the objectives of selling shareholders, the next issue for many ESOPs becomes financing. Can the company, in fact, borrow sufficient funds to acquire stock from the selling shareholders? If the financing burden is too heavy for the company to bear, there are a number of strategies to consider to make the ESOP feasible.

✔ **Seller Financing**   To the extent that bank financing is not available to acquire all of the shares offered to the ESOP, one alternative to consider is seller financing. That is, the selling shareholder holds a note from the ESOP for some or all of the transaction amount. If a bank provides some of the debt, the seller note will normally be subordinated to a loan from a financial institution to the ESOP. This approach, however, usually must be complimented with a second loan that the selling shareholder makes against the qualified replacement property (QRP). This is because the selling shareholder, to qualify for the tax-free rollover, must reinvest the proceeds of the ESOP sale in QRP during the period from 3 months before to 12 months after the sale to the ESOP. Therefore, if all a seller had is a note for some of the stock sold to the ESOP, the seller would typically be unable to acquire the equivalent amount of QRP. Individuals who have other liquid assets, or assets that can be liquidated without adverse tax consequences, would be in a position to acquire QRP without taking a second loan. For most sellers, however, the second loan will be necessary.

Example: the ESOP transaction is for $10 million, representing a 30% stake in the corporation. The bank agrees to loan $8 million. It requires as collateral for the loan the shares in the ESOP, the assets of the corporation not already pledged as collateral, and $4 million of the sellers' QRP. The seller finances the remainder of the transaction by borrowing $2 million against the $4 million QRP that is unencumbered and buying an additional $2 million of QRP. "Floating Rate Notes," marketed by many of the major investment banking firms, can be "margined" (borrowed against) up to 90% or more of their value.

✔ **Newly Issued Stock**   Another alternative to solving the financing issue is the sale of newly issued stock to the ESOP. The sale of newly issued stock to the ESOP can be in combination with the sale by existing shareholders or newly issued shares separately. The sale of these newly issued shares count in determining the percentage of stock owned by the ESOP and thus can be used to partially satisfy the 30% requirement needed for the tax-free rollover. At the same time, newly issued shares sold to the ESOP generate working capital for the company. This working capital can be used for expansion, for repaying existing debt, etc. If the company cannot, and its lenders will not, fund the level of debt needed to finance an ESOP transaction and still meet the 30% threshold, this approach can be the solution, and often is. In fact, the largest closely held company ESOP transaction in 1998, for approximately $75 million, employed this approach.

Of course, issuing new shares means dilution. Thus the current shareholders and the company's board of directors must get comfortable with the level of dilution that is caused by the issuance of new stock. In some circumstances the dilutive impact can be reduced by the use of a convertible preferred stock, but this also complicates the capital structure of the company.

The ultimate test of the dilutive impact of the new share issuance is determined by the return on capital the company ultimately receives. In the words of a former finance professor, "If the company uses the capital to build a Mustang, the shareholders will be very pleased that they were diluted, but if the company builds an Edsel, the shareholders will have quite a different attitude!"

Above (or Below) the Contribution Limit

While it is normally understood that other qualified retirement plans, such as a 401(k) plan, must be taken into account when calculating the 25%-of-payroll contribution limit for ESOPs, there are some other assumptions that are made that may be erroneous.

✔ **Interest Exclusion**   In C corporations, interest is normally excluded from the 25%-of-payroll limit when contributions are made to repay ESOP debt. However, for this exclusion to apply, the company must pass a special discrimination test referred to as the "one-third" test. If the test would otherwise be failed, the eligible payroll of highly compensated employees (HCEs) can be limited in order to pass the test. However, this "limit" solution cannot always fix the problem, because if there is a high level of payroll to highly compensated employees (currently $90,000 and above), capping the payroll of HCEs may reduce the overall payroll to a point where contributions to the adjusted lower payroll will exceed 25% even when interest is excluded. In addition, contributions to repay interest on ESOP debt in an S corporation are not excluded from the 25% limitation.

✔ **Above 25%**   More than one potential ESOP has died an unnecessary death, or come close to it, because of a lack of understanding of how contributions significantly in excess of 25% of covered payroll can be made to the ESOP.

As discussed above, interest is excluded from the 25% limit in C corporations if the "one-third" test is passed. To the extent that 25% is still insufficient to service loan principal, dividends are the answer. Reasonable C corporation dividends can be paid on stock held by an ESOP. To the extent that the dividends are paid on stock acquired with the proceeds of an ESOP loan, those dividends may be used to repay the ESOP debt used to acquire those shares. Additionally, such dividends are excluded from the 25% of payroll limitation and are tax deductible for C corporations. Reasonableness of C corporation dividends is determined by a number of factors, including industry averages and return on investment. However, if the ESOP were to own a convertible preferred stock, the dividend would be determined primarily by the market indicators, i.e., a typical dividend being paid on similar issues of preferred stock. If, for example, the ESOP appraiser determines that for the preferred stock to be valued at par, it needs to pay a 6% dividend, and the value of the preferred stock held by the ESOP is $1 million, then the preferred stock would pay a $60,000 per year preferred dividend that would be excluded from the 25% of payroll limitation.

Also, the IRS stated in Private Letter Ruling 200436015 (June 9, 2004) that the 25% limit on contributions to repay the principal on a leveraged ESOP's loan in a C corporation was separate from the 25% limit for contributions to other qualified defined contribution plans. (This applies only to C corporations.)

S corporation dividends or "distributions" also can be used to repay ESOP debt and are not currently restricted by "reasonableness," as in C corporations. These distributions are also excluded from the contribution limits, often helping a company overcome the 25% of payroll limitation, but S corporation distributions are not tax-deductible. Distributions paid on allocated financed shares may now be used to repay ESOP debt, but if the S distribution has already been allocated, it cannot be used to repay ESOP debt. Any cash in the ESOP derived from previous S corporation distributions paid on allocated, leveraged ESOP shares may be used by the trust to satisfy the ESOP repurchase obligation or to purchase treasury shares from the corporation, as a result of the American Jobs Creation Act of 2004. Because S corporation distributions on leveraged stock can be used to repay ESOP debt, ESOP contributions in some S corporations may be considerably less than those required for equivalent C corporation transactions.

Costs

Costs are sometimes cited as a reason not to do an ESOP. While costs should certainly be considered and understood before undertaking an ESOP, they are rarely a barrier for profitable companies with 50 or more employees.

✔ **The Cost of an ESOP Versus That of Selling to an Outsider**
In evaluating ESOP costs, it is also important to look at the cost of alternatives. As in any other service area, there is a range of fees associated with selling a company through a business broker. One of the largest national firms specializing in the sale of privately held companies charges an initial fee of approximately $30,000, and then a sliding scale of 10% of the first $1 million of sale proceeds, 8% of the second million, 6% of the third million, etc. Other firms may not charge any initial fees, and the percentage of the sale price may be as low as 2% or 3% for multi-million dollar transactions. A bigger consideration may be opportunity costs. There is no guarantee that listing a company for sale will achieve the desired results. What is almost certainly guaranteed is that sooner or later key executives will learn that the company is for sale, and they may start shopping their

services. Several years ago, one large national firm indicated that it was successful in selling approximately 10% of the firms that are listed. On the other hand, if you can identify a strategic buyer in your industry that is a perfect "fit" for your company, or if you know from prior offers that there is interest in acquiring your company, you may be able to confidentially explore the transaction.

If you do receive an offer, it may not necessarily be a lump-sum cash payment. Offers typically involve some sort of down payment and then ongoing payments, sometimes contingent upon future performance. The buyer may require the continued involvement of selling shareholders for a specified period of time, or on the other hand, may require their immediate departure.

The smaller the company, the more difficult it may be to sell to an outsider. On the other hand, if a company is too small (typically less than 20 employees) it is probably too small for an ESOP. However, profitable S corporations may well be able to successfully install an ESOP with fewer employees because of large cash distributions that are typically paid into the trust and are not restricted by payroll limitations.

Even if the offer is a cash lump-sum payment, what will the seller net after paying capital gains taxes, compared to selling to the ESOP and avoiding capital gains taxes (assuming the seller is eligible for the tax-free rollover)?

✔ **Ongoing Costs** Occasionally we see the "tail wag the dog." That is, companies fear the ongoing costs of operating an ESOP. In fact, operating an ESOP requires the same level of expenditure as operating just about any other qualified retirement plan, including a 401(k) plan, plus an annual independent appraisal. Costs for the independent appraisal usually range from $10,000 to $25,000 per year and even more for large or complex situations. However, for most closely held companies the annual appraisal cost will definitely be in the lower end of the range.

✔ **Implementation Costs** This is definitely the area where considerably greater cost is incurred versus other types of retirement plans. Executives today are most familiar with 401(k) plans, where prototype plans are the norm. Because banks and insurance companies aggressively seek to manage the money of employee participants in such plans, they subsidize other services. Unless such a "subsidy" exists through ESOP service firms seeking to provide ongoing recordkeeping services, or manage the investment portfolio of selling shareholder, fund repurchase liability with insurance products, then the true costs of implementing an ESOP will be charged by the practitioners involved in the implementation. As a result, the cost of implementing a leveraged ESOP in a small company, including an *independent* stock appraisal, feasibility study, legal documents, and employee communications, could exceed $60,000, although costs will vary with the experience of the consultants involved and the complexity of the transaction. Larger and more complex ESOP transactions could move into the six-figure area. On the other side of the cost ledger, some companies have employed a "do it yourself" approach and reduced their costs.

The Formal ESOP Feasibility Study

Many companies considering ESOP feasibility determine rather quickly that it is a "go or no go." That is, they decide, after speaking to one or two advisors, that either the ESOP will definitely work for them or it definitely will not work. On many occasions over the course of the past 20 years, we have seen these assumptions prove to be erroneous upon close examination. Even companies that have had ESOPs for a period of years and who may be contemplating a second stage transaction will sometimes miss a key point. That "point" can turn out to make all the difference in the world.

Many corporate advisors recommend that some form of ESOP feasibility analysis be performed when a board of directors, management, and shareholders are considering either installing a new ESOP or contemplating a major transaction in an existing ESOP company. These advisors contend that a comprehensive feasibility study provides a "decision package" for the board and its professional advisors to use as a blueprint for an informed decision regarding the ESOP.

A feasibility study will allow corporate decision-makers to determine if, and to what extent, an ESOP can assist the board, management, and shareholders in achieving desired objectives. Both the technical and practical factors are measured. On the technical side, factors such as ESOP contribution limits, the existence of other qualified retirement plans (such as 401(k) plans) and their relationship with the ESOP, and the company's current status as a C corporation or an S corporation must be carefully examined. On the practical side, factors such as the company's projected cash flow and its ability to repay ESOP debt (if a leveraged ESOP is envisioned), the lender's collateral requirements, and the projected repurchase obligation of the ESOP versus the company's future cash flow projections must also be carefully reviewed.

Is an external ESOP feasibility study (as opposed to an internal, or "do it yourself" study) really necessary? It depends primarily on whether the parties to the decision can definitively and authoritatively answer a number of questions.

Below are questions that address most, but not necessarily all, of the important issues that determine the feasibility of an ESOP or a "second stage" ESOP transaction. These issues and the many more outlined below will determine whether or not a company needs an external feasibility study.

Transaction Design Characteristics

1. **What is the target percentage of stock for the ESOP to acquire?** This is sometimes driven by the desire of selling shareholders in C corporations to qualify for the Code Section 1042 "tax-free" rollover, which requires that the ESOP own a minimum of 30% of the outstanding stock of the corporation after the acquisition. The need to buy out specific shareholders or to avoid selling stock at a minority discount also may affect the target percentage to be acquired by the ESOP.

2. **When will the stock be acquired?** Frequently, ESOPs "warehouse" cash contributions for a relatively short period of time before the ESOP acquires stock. However, loan pro-

ceeds must be used immediately by the ESOP to acquire stock. Many ESOPs purchase shares in two or three stages over a period of five to ten years or more.

3. Will the stock be paid for in a lump sum or in installments?

4. Will this be a leveraged or non-leveraged transaction?
— If leveraged, what is the preferred length of the loan?
If the ESOP is leveraged (i.e., a loan is made from a bank or other financial institution, the corporation sponsoring the ESOP, or selling shareholders) the lender normally will require repayment over a period of five to ten years. (The company-to-ESOP loan may be for a longer term than the bank-to-company loan.) Some or all of the qualified replacement property (QRP) (from a C corporation Section 1042 transaction) or other securities may be required as collateral for the loan. Immediately following the consummation of the ESOP transaction, the per-share fair market value of the stock may drop due to the new ESOP debt that the company has incurred. Individuals seeking to sell stock shortly after a leveraged ESOP transaction has been consummated should be aware of this possibility.

— Who sells what percentage?
Where there are multiple owners, if one owner sells first in a leveraged ESOP transaction, the other owners may see at least a short-term decline in their stock value.

— Will there be more sales to the ESOP in the future?
Considering the possible timing of future sales to the ESOP following the first transaction may well influence the design of the transaction and duration of the financing between the company and the trust. Future sales to the ESOP are desirable in that they tend to even out the contributions to the trust and should lessen the possibility of inequitable future allocations of stock to newer employees.

— Which transaction design yields the greatest tax savings?
Accelerating ESOP contributions reduces taxable income but increases the benefit expense to the corporation due to

the fact that ESOP shares would normally be allocated more rapidly to the accounts of ESOP participants. Additionally, for a closely held company, the ESOP repurchase obligation would become an issue sooner than it would otherwise. The transaction design with the greatest tax saving is not always the most desirable. Allocating too many shares to participants in a relatively short time frame sometimes leads to an unfortunate situation of two classes of employees—those who were present at the first transaction with large ESOP accounts and employees who joined later, after the loan was repaid, with smaller accounts (see Questions 30 and 36 below).

— *How does the transaction design affect benefit policy?*
A quicker repayment of the loan means employees at the early stage of the ESOP may get higher levels of benefits than employees at a later stage. By spreading out payments, contributions can be more balanced over time, but tax benefits would be delayed.

— *Is a control premium applicable?*
If the ESOP will acquire initially, or has the option to acquire in a few years, more than 50% of the company's stock, then a control premium would normally be applied.

— *Will the accounting treatment of ESOP debt cause the company to violate existing loan covenants or create bonding problems?*
Generally accepted accounting principles (GAAP) require that the full amount of the ESOP debt be a reduction to the company's book value.

— *What is the accounting expense to be recognized by the company when it repays an ESOP loan, and why is it different from the cash expense?*
Accounting expense that must be recognized in a leveraged ESOP under GAAP is the fair market value of the shares released from the ESOP suspense account in a given year. The amount of cash contributed by the corporation to repay ESOP principal is ignored in computing the GAAP expense,

and the GAAP expense can differ significantly from the tax expense.

— *Will the accounting treatment of the ESOP debt have an unacceptable effect on bonding, other needs, or loan covenants?*
The financial statement impact of the ESOP is of particular concern to companies that are publicly traded, are contemplating an IPO, or need bonding.

— *Should the company use the fair market value or the cost basis of shares to determine the size of its annual addition to employee accounts?*
The plan can specify either method or can call for using the lower of the cost basis or fair market value

5. **If this is a closely held C corporation, which shareholders qualify for the Code Section 1042 tax-deferred rollover?**
Some stockholders may not be eligible for the tax-deferred rollover.

6. **Can the ESOP buy the target percentage based on:**
— *Cash flow?*
That is, can the company afford to fund the ESOP purchases?

— *Internal Revenue Code contribution limits?*
Contribution limits are normally 25% of covered payroll but can be more or less depending on a number of variables. Company contributions to any other defined contribution plans, such as profit sharing or 401(k) plans, reduce the contribution limit. This includes corporate contributions but not employee deferrals to 401(k) plans. Interest is normally excluded from the 25% of payroll limitation in a leveraged C corporation ESOP when the company passes a special discrimination test. "Reasonable" dividends on common or preferred stock in C corporations as well as S corporation distributions also are excluded from the 25% limitation. Other factors affecting plan contribution levels include the allocation basis (see above), as well as allocating ESOP shares to plan participants at a slower rate than would normally occur due to the repayment of ESOP debt. The issue

of contribution limits is a complex area which can make or break the feasibility of an ESOP.

— Classes of stock?

The ESOP must own either the best class of common stock as to voting and dividend rights, convertible preferred stock that converts to the best class of common, or any class of publicly traded common stock. Convertible preferred stock may be used because the larger dividend (compared to common stock) that can be paid on convertible preferred may be necessary due to Internal Revenue Code contribution limits (see above). Convertible preferred stock could be counter-dilutive for stockholders outside of the ESOP. "Super common" stock is sometimes a viable alternative to convertible preferred stock if an adequate investor rate of return in multi-investor ESOP transactions is a critical issue. As will be seen later, S corporations are limited to one class of stock.

— Other shareholder or management concerns?

These could include passing some percentage of stock to other individuals, maintaining a certain percentage of stock ownership in the hands of certain shareholders, or the unwillingness of enough shareholders to sell the ESOP a 30% stake.

— Availability of capital for growth and expansion?

The debt that the corporation is repaying in a leveraged ESOP can reduce or eliminate any additional debt capacity. As a result, debt capital to expand, acquire other companies, etc., may not be available when needed. As ESOP debt is repaid, shares are allocated to accounts of ESOP participants, which means a growing repurchase obligation for a closely held company. If this repurchase obligation is not properly anticipated and planned for, funds that would otherwise be used for growth and expansion may be claimed by the "buyback" obligations that the company has for participants who retire, die, become disabled, terminate for other reasons (see below), or become eligible for diversification at age 55 with 10 years of participation in the ESOP.

— Are other sources of ESOP capital available?
These sources can include the use of the assets of other qualified retirement plans, such as profit sharing plans; wage reductions; or employee investments through a 401(k)/ESOP. All of these approaches introduce a considerable degree of complexity and additional fiduciary risk to the ESOP equation.

Plan Design Details

7. **Who, if anyone, is excluded from the ESOP?** Selling shareholders electing the "tax-free" rollover are excluded from ESOP participation, along with certain family members and 25% shareholders. Part-time employees are normally excluded but do not have to be. Certain classes of employees and union members may or may not be excluded depending on a number of variables. Employees who are members of a bargaining unit that bargains for retirement benefits may be excluded from participation in the ESOP. (An ESOP, like any other qualified retirement plan, can be the subject of collective bargaining.) Occasionally, small percentages of non-union employees who are in a separate line of work, perhaps in a subsidiary company, are excluded from participation in the ESOP. Any employee with less than 1,000 hours in a year or less than one year of service can be excluded. Companies may want to expand the rules for eligible employees to increase eligible payroll, which in turn increases contribution limits. In some plans, expanded eligibility may be cut back after a few years if the plan specifies this at the outset.

8. **How can sellers and family members excluded from ESOP participation be "made whole"?** Nonqualified deferred compensation agreements can be used for this purpose. The corporation promises to pay a supplemental retirement benefit to individuals who are excluded from the ESOP.

9. **What happens to the:**
    — 401(k) plan, if any?
    401(k) plans should be retained if at all possible because they provide a cushion of diversification for ESOP participants and build a stronger retirement posture for all employees.

— Profit sharing plan, if any?
Contributions to profit sharing plans are normally shifted to the ESOP.

— Defined benefit pension plan, if any?
While defined benefit plans are much less common than they used to be, such a plan may stay in place along with the ESOP under certain circumstances.

10. **Voting rights**   ESOP participants have limited required voting rights in closely held companies, but companies can go beyond these if desired. Current shareholders may or may not be willing to share additional voting rights with ESOP participants, such as voting for the board of directors.

11. **Other ESOP design features, including:**
    — Vesting
    Vesting must be completed in five years (for "cliff" vesting) or seven years (for "graded" vesting). Should credit be given for prior service?

    — Distribution alternatives
    Deferring ESOP distributions and/or making ESOP installment distributions over the maximum periods allowed by law will reduce for a period of time the cash necessary to meet a closely held company's repurchase obligation. However, for a company whose stock is growing in value, this policy ultimately increases the cost of the repurchase obligation. Many companies attempt to balance the cash flow requirements of early distributions with a policy that accelerates to some extent ESOP distributions, especially after some or all of any ESOP acquisition debt has been repaid.

    — Allocation formula
    The "normal" ESOP allocation formula is based strictly on covered compensation, with the current maximum allowed by law of $205,000 per year. Alternatives include a formula that gives some credit for prior service, combined with additional points for compensation.

12. **Do competitors have ESOPs?** If there is a strong track record of ESOP performance in your industry, it will be much easier to gauge how you might expect the ESOP to perform from a motivational perspective.

13. **Do employees in this industry expect to be equity owners?** If so, will what they get from the ESOP be sufficient? Will certain employees need additional ownership?

14. **Are there union employees? If so, will they be treated the same as all other employees or differently?** Union members usually may be excluded from the ESOP. An ESOP, like all other qualified retirement plans, is subject to collective bargaining, however (see Question 7 above).

Management Incentives

15. **Will there be additional stock incentives for management?** If so, will such incentives take the form of stock options, a stock bonus, a stock purchase plan, stock appreciation rights (SARs), restricted stock, or a combination of one or more of the above? Frequently, an ESOP is paired with one or more of these equity-based incentive plans to maximize equity incentives for employees. Will any of these incentives be in conflict with the anti-abuse provisions under Code Section 409(p) and the regulations issued by the IRS related to S corporation ESOP companies? See Question 37 below.

16. **What other nonqualified plans (such as nonqualified deferred compensation) will be coordinated with the ESOP?** The existence of the ESOP does not prevent the company from continuing existing nonqualified plans or implementing new ones. Frequently, nonqualified deferred compensation plans are implemented to cover those that are excluded under the Section 1042 "tax-free" rollover rules.

17. **What is the long-term impact of dilution, if any, of these plans?** By definition, dilution occurs any time that new stock is issued. Quasi-equity plans such as stock apprecia-

tion rights (SARs) or phantom stock are not dilutive, although they do reduce company earnings. The impact of any equity appreciation plan on the per-share value of the stock should be carefully considered.

Fiduciary and ESOP Management Issues

18. **Will the ESOP trustee be "internal"?** Most ESOP companies "self-trustee" their plans. Various individuals who are stockholders and/or employees serve as trustees. There are fiduciary responsibilities and risks associated with serving as an ESOP trustee, however, which may justify the cost of outside fiduciaries. Potential conflicts of interest can arise. And sellers to an ESOP should never be trustees acting on behalf of the ESOP at the time when the ESOP transaction is consummated.

19. **If external, will the ESOP trustee be independent or directed?** An institutional trustee may be directed as to the voting of the shares held in trust. An ESOP committee, which may be appointed by the board, elected in some manner, or some combination of the two, would direct the trustee as to the voting of the shares in the ESOP. Both the trustee and the ESOP committee bear fiduciary responsibility unless an independent fiduciary is directing them.

20. **If independent, will the trustee serve for the transaction only or both for the transaction and on an ongoing basis?** Independent institutional ESOP trustees may be appointed by the board of directors for a specific ESOP transaction, either the initial ESOP purchase of stock, a subsequent purchase of stock, or the sale of stock by an ESOP. Except for these specific transactions, individuals are frequently appointed by the board to serve as trustees.

21. **If the trustee is directed, will shareholders/management serve as the ESOP committee?** The ESOP committee normally directs the trustee as to voting shares held in the ESOP.

22. Who will be the:

- Independent valuation firm?

- ESOP attorney?

- ESOP lender (if this is a leveraged ESOP)?

- ESOP administrator?

- ESOP quarterback (coordinator)?

The coordinator may be one of the other parties listed above (such as the attorney) or may be a separate advisor.

23. What role will the following professional advisors play:

- Corporate attorney?

- Personal attorney?

- Accountant?

- Insurance agent?

- Investment banker?

- Benefit consultant?

- Other advisors?

24. Who will prepare the ESOP communications plan? The initial ESOP communications program is often a joint effort between an ESOP consultant and the company's top leaders, supported by the Human Resources department. Companies usually assign one energetic and respected individual to be responsible for ongoing ESOP communications. Many ESOP companies enlist the aid of communication specialists, either on an ongoing basis, or at specific times.

25. When and where will employee communications occur? Announcing an ESOP should be a special celebration with spouses in attendance if possible. Many companies take employees off-site or have the meetings held after hours. Remote office locations are a special challenge. Videotapes and videoconferencing are two frequently used tools.

The ESOP Repurchase Obligation

26. **What are the repurchase obligation projections for death, disability, retirement, diversification and "other" terminations for the next 10 to 15 years?** A careful study of this obligation often influences the percentage of ownership of the company by the ESOP.

27. **Can the company handle the obligation and still maintain desired growth?** Too large a repurchase obligation in proportion to available cash flow can stifle a company's ability to modernize and compete in the long term.

28. **Is the percentage of distributions to other terminations— i.e., those who quit or are fired—too high?**
 — *If yes, what measures will reduce this problem?*
Proper design of ESOP eligibility criteria, such as entry age and vesting schedules, and a deferred and/or installment distribution policy can assist, but the root problem may require careful study of the company's retention system.

29. **How can the cost of the repurchase obligation be reduced or "smoothed"?** In many cases, a closely held company is wise to adopt a policy that defers, to an appropriate extent, the payout from one to six years for other terminations. This "smoothes" (evens out) cash flow and precludes a situation wherein employees with large ESOP accounts are tempted to "take the money and run." The ESOP rules pertaining to other terminations allow companies to wait six years before payments must begin, and then balances can be paid out in equal annual installments over a five-year period. However, if a company's stock price is rising faster than its after-tax cost of money, delaying repurchase only increases the cost. Thus the company must balance the need to defer distributions long enough so as not to tempt vested employees to leave to receive a benefit payment against the need to begin the payout process soon enough in order to reduce the long-term costs.

30. **Will the repurchase obligation be funded? If so, how and when?** Many closely held companies will fund their repurchase obligations from annual cash flow by contributing on a tax-deductible basis the necessary cash to the ESOP to distribute cash to departing participants. This approach relies on the uncertainty of future cash flow. It also causes the ESOP repurchase obligation to grow as the repurchased shares are allocated to the remaining participants' accounts. This can create problems for established ESOP companies in which two classes of ESOP participants emerge: some with large account balances, some with small.

    The decision in a given year whether to redeem departing participant shares back to the corporation, or recycling shares within the ESOP has long-term implications of counter-dilution for the non-ESOP shareholders, taxes to the company, and the ultimate size of the ESOP. A detailed analysis of stockholder equity and ESOP repurchase obligation quantifies the differences.

    A corporate funding plan that establishes tax-deferred reserves on the balance sheet to address this obligation is a wise decision—the sooner, the better. Properly structured life insurance programs can be very effective in meeting this obligation. This funding plan can frequently be integrated in a manner that facilitates shareholder estate plans as well as key executive requirements.

    In S corporations, as explained in the next section, there may be a buildup of cash resulting from tax savings and other distributions into the trust that will greatly facilitate ESOP repurchase planning.

Special S Corporation ESOP Considerations

31. **What is the long-range impact of tax savings in an S versus C corporation ESOP?** Analysis has shown that the long-term tax savings generated by S corporation ESOP companies can be significantly greater than for some C corporations.

    ESOPs in S corporations currently offer no Section 1042 tax deferred sale opportunity and are subject to reduced limits on the tax-deductible amounts that can be contributed to the ESOP. There are also limitations on the amount of ESOP distributions that may be used to pay down the acquisition loan. But these drawbacks are mitigated by several factors. Because the ESOP's portion of stock owned in an S corporation is exempt from federal (and most state) income taxes, a profitable company may use these savings to make ESOP distributions to the trust that are not restricted by "reasonableness." This will often offset the lower deductible limits and can result in an ESOP loan being repaid faster than for a C corporation. In some companies, large ESOP accounts for selling shareholders will offset the absence of Section 1042 sale tax savings.

32. How much, if any, of company income must be distributed to the ESOP? The ESOP must receive its proportional share of all S corporation distributions made to shareholders.

— What uses may the ESOP trustees select for the large cash distributions that may accumulate in the trust?
The ESOP may use a portion of these funds for the retirement of an ESOP loan, the acquisition of more ESOP shares either from the company (to create capital) or from shareholders, the ESOP repurchase obligation, and/or taxable cash payments to employees to help them feel more like true co-owners of the company.

— How can these funds promote company and shareholder objectives?
A carefully developed plan can maximize the use of savings in a manner that will balance the sometimes-competing objectives between different shareholders.

33. What will the future value of the shareholders' accumulated adjustment (AA) accounts be? The fact that shareholders retain individual accumulated adjustments accounts—representing their share of retained earnings on which they have already paid taxes—is a desirable benefit of the S corporate structure. Since the board may make pro-rata distributions to shareholders at any time, avoiding any further taxation, it is important to track the value of these accounts for major shareholders as part of the long term stockholders' equity analysis.

34. **Will stock be voting and/or nonvoting?** S corporations are generally restricted to holding only one class of stock. However, with proper design, it may be possible to permit both voting and non-voting stock so as to achieve particular objectives of the shareholder(s) and the corporation.

35. **What are the effects of the built-in gains and LIFO recapture taxes compared to the tax savings available to S corporation ESOPs?** Depending upon a particular C corporation's accounting methods, and if and when the C corporation is sold, making the S election may not result in significant additional taxes. A thorough multi-year stockholder equity analysis will illustrate whether the special tax savings available to an S corporation will outweigh these costs. Our experience after studying numerous S corporation ESOP transactions is that few companies find these taxes so onerous as to preclude an otherwise advantageous transition to S corporation status.

36. **What are the implications of the selected plan on the possibility of creating two categories of employees over the long term, i.e., the "haves" and the "have-nots"?** Because of the special features and tax savings associated with S corporation ESOPs, if a company does not plan for the long run, serious imbalances could occur in stock accounts among new versus older employee groups. Established C corporation ESOPs have managed this problem for many years, some more effectively than others, but the challenge can be greater for the S corporation, especially if large S distributions will be made to the ESOP.

37. **What is the impact of recent S corporation legislation?** Legislation enacted in 1998 for the first time permitted an S corporation to sponsor an ESOP that acquires company stock. In 2001, President George W. Bush signed into law the Economic Growth and Tax Relief Reconciliation Act, which,

among many other positive tax and qualified plan changes, eliminated potential loopholes allowing S corporation ESOPs to be set up just to benefit a small group of selling owners and other individuals. These changes generally apply only to small companies. However, the anti-abuse provisions of Code Section 409(p), combined with subsequent IRS regulations, must be carefully studied before a final decision can be made regarding an S corporation ESOP.

The answers to most of the questions above relating to S corporations can come only from a comprehensive financial analysis.

Creating an Ownership Culture

38. **What is the importance of creating an ownership culture in an employee-owned company?** Although the answers to all 38 questions are important, the question pertaining to how well the management-employee team is effecting the culture change within the organization may provide the biggest payoff to ESOP companies. Some companies install an ESOP primarily for financial reasons such as a tax-deferred sale for shareholders and tax-favored financing for the company. Many of these companies never develop the partnering message of the risks and rewards to complement the rights and responsibilities of stock ownership. Research indicates that those companies that have effectively communicated employee ownership—thereby creating and enhancing an ownership culture among employees—have reaped the greatest success from their ESOP strategy.

Most ESOP companies eventually make some progress in communicating the impact of employee ownership. However, stellar ESOP companies achieve their full potential by creating a long-term ownership culture, stimulating creativity and innovation among all participants. The psychological reward for employees whose personal innovations and ideas have been recognized by all to improve the organization is quite immediate and contagious.

Conclusion

There you have it. Once you have answered all the above-listed questions, plus some others that your corporate attorney, accountant, or other key advisor(s) will raise, you do not need a feasibility study! However, if you are unable to answer these critical questions, a feasibility study will provide the basis for a sound decision on an ESOP strategy or transaction that will truly facilitate shareholder and company objectives.

CHAPTER 5

HOW SMALL IS TOO SMALL FOR AN ESOP?

COREY ROSEN

One of the most frequently asked questions we receive at the National Center for Employee Ownership is "Am I too small to have an ESOP?" There is no simple answer. There are, however, some basic guidelines that can help determine whether an ESOP is worthwhile.

First, of course, you must know how much an ESOP will cost. Unfortunately, cost estimates vary widely from one case to another and one consultant to another. There are several components of cost—preparing plan documents and government filings; obtaining a valuation; administration; and, in a leveraged ESOP, loan commitment fees, legal fees for the lender's counsel and loan documents, and, possibly, financial consulting for structuring the transaction.

The cost of drawing up the plan documents and government filings is generally not as much as people think it will be. In a small company transaction, legal fees of $10,000 or more are typical. These costs will be somewhat lower if you come well prepared, already understanding the basics of ESOP rules and knowing what you want your plan to do. Most ESOP attorneys have plan document templates in their word processing systems. Their fees are largely a function of the time they spend with you figuring out what the document should include.

Valuation normally will carry fees in the same range for smaller companies, assuming that there is only one class of stock in the company and no unusual complicating elements.

Repeat annual valuations should be about half this fee. It may be possible to obtain an even lower fee in some cases, but it is imperative that costs not be cut by hiring people who do not normally do ESOP work.

Plan administration costs—e.g., keeping records, filing reports, and sending plan account statements—depend on the number of employees. There are certain fixed costs, however, so there are some economies of scale for larger companies. A company of 20 employees might reasonably expect to pay around $2,000 per year as a base cost, plus $30 to $60 per employee.

Costs become really high when an ESOP borrows money. The lender usually wants legal opinions from its counsel, charges loan commitment fees, and needs loan documents prepared, not unlike the fees involved in a mortgage transaction. Even in a transaction of several hundred thousand dollars, this could add another $10,000 or more to the costs. If a loan cannot easily be obtained, or if the transaction involves multiple sources of financing, it may be necessary to hire a financial adviser to help structure the deal. These experts often charge a percentage of the transaction costs, typically 1% to 3%, with the percentage a function of the size of the transaction.

All of these estimates should be viewed cautiously. Invariably, when we report costs we receive at least a few complaints that we misled people. Some say our estimates are much too high; some say much too low. The truth is that costs vary considerably depending on the nature of the transaction. The costs listed here are "ballpark" numbers for simple transactions.

Assessing Costs Versus Benefits

There are several things to consider when trying to figure out if these costs can be justified:

✔ **What Are the Alternatives?** It will probably cost $40,000 or more for a leveraged ESOP to buy out part or all of an owner's interest in a 20-employee company. That may seem exorbitant in, say, a $500,000 sale. But what are the choices?

If the company is sold by a business broker, a percentage of the fee will be charged that will at least match that. If a partial interest is for sale, it may be difficult or impossible to find another buyer willing to offer a reasonable price, adequate security, or a satisfactory continuing employment relationship if the seller wants to stay with the company. Employers also may have a strong preference to have employees own the company.

✔ **What Is Your Tax Bracket?**   If you are not paying taxes or are in a low tax bracket, some tax advantages may have little application, although the rollover benefits may still be worthwhile to the seller.

✔ **How Will Annual Costs Compare to Annual Contributions?** The annual fees you pay, including an amortized amount for start-up costs, should be less than the amount of annual contributions you make multiplied by your tax rate (e.g., if your costs are $9,000 per year and your combined federal-state tax rate is 30%, you should be able to contribute at least $30,000 per year). Otherwise, you might consider a non-tax-qualified plan.

✔ **Is Your Payroll Adequate?**   Figure out what the eligible payroll of the people actually in your plan will be (exclude pay of people who will not qualify for participation or an individual's pay over $205,000 a year [as of 2004]). Then multiply that by 25%. In a leveraged plan, multiply this number times the number of years of the loan, and this will give you an estimate of the maximum amount you can borrow. Is this going to be enough of an annual contribution to buy as much stock as you want to make available?

As a rule of thumb, ESOPs work best for companies with over 20 employees, but a little back-of-the-envelope calculating using the above formulas can give you a much better idea.

S Corporation Issues

For S corporations interested in ESOPs, there are special considerations in determining who is too small for an ESOP.

The 2001 tax law included provisions to prevent a small group of employees from abusing the exemption from federal income tax for income attributable to an ESOP in an S corporation. Prior to this law, some companies were setting up ESOPs, for instance, where a management group was spun off to a separate S corporation. A handful of employees would then become participants in the plan, while the operating company's employees would remain in a C corporation without a plan. The management group would charge very large fees to the operating company, declare those as profits, and pay no tax on them. Alternatively, a small group of professionals might set up an ESOP as a means of avoiding income tax.

To prevent such abuses, Congress passed legislation that creates punitive taxes for S corporation ESOPs that provide benefits only to a small number of employees. The law is complex. It is described in detail in the NCEO's book *S Corporation ESOPs*. One of its consequences is that companies with 10 or fewer employees practically cannot do an S corporation ESOP. Even somewhat larger companies may find it difficult without careful planning. As companies get larger than 15 or so employees, however, it becomes increasingly practical. Of course, small companies can still implement a C corporation ESOP if they are already C corporations or switch from S status.

6

A Practical Approach to ESOP Contribution and Allocation Limits

Scott Rodrick
David R. Johanson

One of the most important matters that a company should consider when analyzing the feasibility of implementing an ESOP is how much the company can (1) can contribute to an ESOP trust and deduct for corporate income tax purposes and (2) allocate to ESOP participants' accounts. This is particularly an issue in closely held companies where the ESOP trust will purchase a substantial block of capital stock from the owner(s) either in a leveraged transaction where a loan will have to be repaid or when purchases will take place over time as cash resources permit. The company must try to structure the transaction so that the ESOP trust can incur a sufficient amount of debt and purchase the desired amount of capital stock. Alternatively, the company can maximize deductible contributions on an annual basis and orchestrate one or more purchases of capital stock by the ESOP trust as the funds are contributed to the trust. This chapter reviews the primary limits on deductible contributions under Section 404(a)(3), (7), and (9) of the Internal Revenue Code of 1986, as amended (the "Code"), and on annual additions under Section 415(c) of the Code. It also discusses practical ways to work with these limits to achieve a company's goals for its ESOP.[1] This chapter does not address the limitations under applicable state law, which vary greatly.[2]

The Deductible Contribution and Annual Addition Allocation Rules

The Code provides two types of limits on the level of benefits that a company may provide under an ESOP: the limit on overall deductible contributions to the ESOP trust under Section 404 of the Code, and the limit on annual additions (allocations) to an ESOP participant's account under Section 415 of the Code. The Economic Growth and Tax Relief Reconciliation Act of 2001, as amended (EGTRRA), substantially improved these limits for plan years beginning in 2002. This chapter discusses the limits as they now apply and also briefly explains the previous limits to provide a point of reference for older material that may still be in print and that has been discussed in conferences or meetings that readers have attended.

✔ **Section 404 25%–50% Contribution Limit** Section 404(a)(3) of the Code generally limits the total amount of a company's deductible contributions to an ESOP trust and any other defined contribution plans (such as a 401(k) plan or a profit sharing plan) to an amount equal to 25% of eligible payroll each year.[3] Salary reductions by a participant pursuant to a 401(k) plan and/or a 403(b) plan are not taken into account under EGTRRA for purposes of any limitation contained in paragraphs (3), (7), or (9) of Section 404(a) of the Code, and such salary reductions are not taken into account in applying any such limitation to any other contributions and calculating the ceilings that limit how much can be deducted by employers for contributions to employer plans on behalf of employees beginning for plan years after December 31, 2001.[4] Thus, for example, if eligible payroll for all ESOP participants is $1 million per year, the maximum deductible contribution will be $250,000 for all company contributions to all defined contribution plans.

For plan years starting before 2002, the limit for non-leveraged ESOPs and for ESOPs sponsored by S corporations was 15% of eligible payroll unless the ESOP included a money purchase pension plan (i.e., a plan with a fixed contribution feature), in which case the limit increased to 25%. Now, there is generally no reason to add a money purchase pension plan to an ESOP unless it is done to express a contractual commitment to employees (either for collective bargaining purposes or otherwise), because the Section 404 limit is 25% in all situations.[5]

"Eligible payroll" generally refers here to the total compensation reported or reportable on the Form W-2 of all employees eligible to participate in the ESOP and receive allocations of ESOP contributions, omitting the portion of any one person's compensation that is above $205,000 (as of 2004; this limit is indexed for inflation) and that would result in the participant receiving annual additions in the aggregate of more than $41,000 (this limit is also indexed for inflation). Formerly, employee pretax contributions (i.e., salary reductions) to 401(k) plans and Section 125 "cafeteria" plans reduced eligible payroll for tax deduction and contribution purposes; however, as of 2002 this is no longer the case, and these contributions are included in calculating eligible payroll.[6] The compensation of employees that are prohibited by Section 409(n) of the Code from sharing in allocations of company stock in a tax-deferred transaction to which Section 1042 applies (because such employees are the selling owners themselves, are more-than-25% shareholders of the company that issued the stock, or are certain relatives of such individuals[7]) or that are prohibited by Section 409(p) of the Code from sharing in allocations of company stock because of EGTRRA's anti-abuse rule (with respect to an S corporation) also is excluded from eligible payroll in determining deductible contribution limits.[8]

A company may choose to deliberately reduce eligible payroll when designing an ESOP. For example, the ESOP may exclude compensation over an amount that is less than $205,000 (or $164,000—the effective cap on compensation as a result of the annual addition dollar limit of $41,000, which is 25% of $164,000, not $205,000) as a way to spread the ESOP benefit to lower-paid employees (because allocations to ESOP participants' accounts are based on each participant's eligible payroll or something more equitable, lowering the amount of eligible payroll that is counted makes everyone's ESOP benefits more equal). Alternatively, the company may count only regular wages and not commissions or bonuses (similarly, this would prevent higher wage earners from receiving proportionately higher ESOP benefits). A company also may decide to broaden participation in an ESOP by not requiring a minimum number of hours of service or employment on the last day of the plan year in order to receive an allocation. This will generally increase the amount of such an employer's deductible contribution limits under Section 404 of the Code.

Generally, in calculating the Section 404 deductible contribution limits under the Code, all employer (but not employee salary reduction) contributions to defined contribution plans (including ESOPs, profit-sharing plans, 401(k) plans and so on) are taken into account. For example, a company matching contribution pursuant to a 401(k) plan will reduce the amount that can be contributed to an ESOP; however, the company may choose to make the ESOP a combination 401(k)/ESOP (a "KSOP"), in which case the company match is a contribution to the ESOP trust itself. Such a match can be made from the company stock that is released from the ESOP loan suspense account under a leveraged ESOP. This will not decrease the limits on deductible contributions under Section 404 of the Code because the cash contributions that the ESOP trust uses to repay debt also will result in the release of company stock to be used as matching contributions.

Technically speaking, Section 404 of the Code limits not how much can be contributed but only how much can be deducted. If the company contributes more than it can deduct, however, it will be subject to a 10% excise tax on the excess amount.[9] Consequently, the Section 404 limit effectively caps how much a company can contribute in this respect, and ESOP companies generally do not even consider trying to contribute more than they can deduct (although it periodically happens, and then such companies must complete Form 5330 and file it with the IRS to report the nondeductible contribution and pay the applicable excise tax).[10]

In a C corporation, the company itself takes the deduction for income tax purposes, while in an S corporation, the employer contribution reduces the amount of profit on which non-ESOP shareholders must pay income taxes.

In Private Letter Ruling (PLR) 200436015, dated June 9, 2004, the IRS indicated that the 25% deduction limit on employer contributions to repay the principal on an ESOP loan is separate from the 25% limit on employer contributions to other defined contribution plans. Thus, a company could contribute 25% of payroll to repay principal on an ESOP loan while contributing a separate 25% to other plans, for a total 50% limit. (Interest payments on the ESOP loan are outside these limits.) The specific points made in PLR 200436015 include:

1. Section 404(a)(3) of the Code provides for deductible contributions of 25% of eligible payroll pursuant to a money purchase pension plan, a profit sharing plan, and/or a stock bonus plan.

2. Matching contributions pursuant to a 401(k) plan are deductible under Section 404(a)(3) of the Code and are subject to the same maximum 25% limit when aggregated with contributions described in (1) above.

3. Section 404(a)(9)(A) of the Code provides for a *separate and additional deduction* for contributions applied by an ESOP trust to repay the principal of a loan incurred to purchase "qualifying employer securities," subject to a separate 25% limit apart from the limit on contributions provided by Section 404(a)(3) of the Code and described in (1) and (2) above. (This interpretation is what makes the expanded "25% plus 25%" deduction possible.)

4. Section 404(a)(9)(B) of the Code provides for a separate and additional deduction for interest applied by an ESOP to pay interest on a loan described in (3) above; this is not subject to any 25% limit. It is, of course, subject to an ERISA fiduciary limitation in that the ESOP loan interest must be reasonable.

5. For purposes of applying Section 404 of the Code to other contributions, salary reduction contributions under Sec-

tion 402(g) of the Code are not taken into account, and pursuant to Section 404(n) of the Code, the limitations of Sections 404(a)(3), (a)(7), and (a)(9) of the Code do not apply to such salary deferral contributions.

The IRS made it clear that this ruling is based on the assumption that the proposed contributions would otherwise not exceed the annual limitations set forth in Section 415 of the Code (i.e., 100% of eligible compensation or $41,000 [as indexed]).

The ruling in PLR 200436015 is consistent with the ruling in PLR 9548036, in which the IRS ruled that an employer may take a maximum deduction under Section 404(a)(9) of the Code for leveraged ESOP contributions used to make payments of principal and interest on an ESOP loan while simultaneously taking a maximum deduction under Section 404(a)(3) of the Code for contributions to a profit sharing plan. Please remember, however, that a PLR cannot be used as precedent, and subsequent guidance may or may not follow the above-cited PLRs.

Extending the logic of PLR 200436015, it may be conceivable to use the entire 50% of payroll to repay an ESOP loan. This would most likely involve adopting a leveraged ESOP plan and an eligible individual account plan (EIAP), operating the two plans side-by-side and covering the same employees.[11] Every year, the company would contribute an amount equal to 25% of payroll pursuant to each plan, after which the EIAP contribution would be transferred to the ESOP trust to be used in repaying the ESOP loan. However, such an arrangement could be adversely affected by regulatory action on the ground that regardless of the form of the transaction (25% pursuant to a leveraged ESOP and 25% to another defined contribution plan), the substance of the transaction is actually a prohibited 50% contribution to a leveraged ESOP.

Finally, this expanded "25% plus 25%" deduction is available only in C corporations, not S corporations, because Section 404(a)(9)(C) of the Code provides that Section 404(a)(9) of the Code, which is the basis for the separate 25% leveraged ESOP deduction, does not apply to an S corporation.[12]

✔ **Going Above the 25% Contribution Limit** For C corporations, the 25% limit described above is not absolute. First, if PLR 200436015 and PLR 9548036 are followed, it is possible to contribute and deduct up to 50% of eligible payroll pursuant to Sections 404(a)(3) and 404(a)(9) of the Code.

Second, in C corporations,[13] contributions to pay interest on a leveraged ESOP's loan are not included in the 25% limit, provided that not more than one-third of the ESOP contributions are allocated to the ESOP accounts of highly compensated employees.[14] There are creative and legitimate ways to ensure compliance with this one-third test by using deductible dividends under Section 404(k) of the Code (see discussion in next paragraph).

Third, under Section 404 of the Code, dividends that a C corporation's board of directors declares and pays on ESOP trust-held company stock are deductible if the dividends are (1) passed through directly to participants, (2) used to repay a leveraged ESOP trust's loan that was used to buy the shares on which such dividends are paid, or (3) starting in 2002, reinvested in company stock at the direction of participants instead of being passed through to them. To be deductible, dividends must be reasonable and must not constitute "an avoidance or evasion of taxation."[15] In S corporations, earnings on company stock held by an ESOP trust are generally not considered to be dividends but rather are treated as distributions. S corporation distributions of earnings paid on shares of company stock held by an ESOP trust are not tax-deductible under Section 404(k) of the Code. As with C corporations, distributions on both allocated and unallocated shares of company stock can now be used to repay the loan used to acquire such shares.[16]

The timing of the dividend deduction differs depending upon whether the dividends are (1) paid or distributed to the ESOP participant, (2) reinvested in company stock, or (3) are used to repay a leveraged ESOP's loan. With respect to dividends described in (1), the deduction is allowable in the C corporation's taxable year in which the dividends are paid or distributed to an ESOP participant or his or her beneficiary. With respect to dividends described in (2), the new law that makes these types of dividends deductible includes a technical error (a prior reference for the timing of the deduction for dividends described in (3) incorrectly refers to the dividends described in (2)) that does not make it clear when the deduction is allowable. Intuitively, the dividend should be allowable in the C corporation's taxable year in which the dividends would have been distributed to ESOP participants and instead were reinvested in company stock at the direction of such participants. With respect to dividends described in (3), the deduction is allowable in the C corporation's taxable year in which they are used to repay the leveraged ESOP's loan.

✔ **Section 415 Annual Addition Limit** Whereas Section 404 of the Code limits the total yearly contribution that a company may make and deduct for ESOPs and other defined contribution plans, Section 415 of the Code limits the yearly amount of "annual additions" that can be allocated to all of the defined contribution plan accounts of any particular participant. For plan years starting in 2002, these "annual additions" (including employer contributions, any employee salary reduction contributions, and reallocated forfeitures except as described in the next paragraph) cannot exceed the lesser of $41,000 (this figure is indexed for inflation) or 100% of eligible payroll.[17]

For plan years starting before 2002, the Section 415 limits were much lower: the lesser of 25% of eligible payroll (instead of 100%) or a dollar amount that was $30,000 for some years and then reached $35,000 for plan years beginning in 2001. And before 2000, if the employer sponsored a defined benefit plan, it had to be aggregated (via a complex formula) with the ESOP and any other defined contribution plans when calculating annual addition limits.[18]

When ESOP participants leave a company before they are vested, they forfeit the unvested amounts that have been allocated to their accounts. With respect to C corporations, when such forfeitures (1) consist of company stock that the ESOP trust has purchased with the proceeds of a loan and (2) are reallocated to accounts of other ESOP participants, they are not included in the annual addition limits described above, provided that not more than one-third of the contributions to the ESOP trust are allocated to highly compensated employees.[19] As of this time, it is not clear whether Congress intended this special rule to apply to ESOPs maintained by S corporations.

The penalty for exceeding the Section 415 limits is severe: The entire plan is subject to disqualification because compliance with Section 415 of the Code is a requirement for qualification under Section 401(a) of the Code.

Strategies for Dealing with the Limits

Nowadays (for plan years starting in 2002 and thereafter), companies are unlikely to run up against the Section 415 annual addition limit; instead, the Section 404 deductible contribution limit is more likely to be the sticking point. For example, take a company worth $20 million with $1 million in eligible payroll, which means the Section 404 deductible contribution limit would allow only $250,000 per year to be contributed to the ESOP trust. Let us suppose that the company will set up a leveraged ESOP to buy 30% of the company's capital stock from its founders in a transaction to which Section 1042 of the Code applies, allowing the founders to defer recognition of capital gains on the sale. If 30% of the company's capital stock has a fair market value of $6 million (ignoring for purposes of this example minority discounts, lack of marketability discounts, etc., that an independent appraiser might have to apply), then, at $250,000 per year, it would take 24 years to repay the ESOP trust's loan from the company. It is unlikely that a bank would agree to loan such funds to the company under these terms (five- to ten-year loan terms are more typical). This would mean that the company would not be matching its deductible contributions to the ESOP trust with its payments of principal and interest to the external lender and the repayment of principal to the outside lender will have to be made at least partially with after-tax dollars. How can a company deal with this problem?

✔ **Dividends** As noted above, under Section 404(k) of the Code, dividends (or S corporation distributions of earnings on both allocated and unallocated shares of capital stock) can be used to repay an ESOP trust's loan used to buy the shares of company stock on which such dividends (or distributions) are paid.[20] It is not entirely clear whether the nexus between distributions of earnings on S corporation company stock and the use of such distributions to repay an ESOP loan must be maintained in an S corporation ESOP. This requirement is expressly indicated in Section 404(k) of the Code with respect to dividends in a C corporation ESOP. Dividends must be "reasonable." The IRS has not formally defined what is reasonable, but its most recent ESOP examination guidelines[21] identify three separate areas that an independent appraiser and financial adviser for an ESOP trust and/or ESOP fiduciaries must focus on when making this determination: (1) the percentage of eligible payroll that will be allocated to ESOP participants' accounts as a result of the dividend payments; (2) whether the company can continue to declare and pay the same level of dividend payments on an annual and recurring basis; and (3) the extent to which the dividends are comparable to what similarly situated publicly traded companies in the same industry would pay (Section 662 of EGTRRA appears to apply this last analytical approach to the new requirements for the reinvestment and deductibility of dividends under an ESOP). In ruling that a 63% dividend rate was not reasonable, the IRS has stated that to be deductible under Section 404(k) of the Code, dividends must not be greatly in excess of what the company could reasonably be expected to pay on a recurring basis and that a reasonable dividend rate is one "that is normally paid in the ordinary course of business."[22]

In one case, the United States Court of Appeals for the Eighth Circuit affirmed a United States Tax Court decision that the IRS may recharacterize unreasonably high dividends as annual additions to the ESOP participants' accounts, which, in turn, may cause the Section 415 limits to be exceeded, and lead to the disqualification of the ESOP.[23] Just because a dividend is in the upper range of what comparable securities would pay, however, does not make it unreasonable for purposes of Section 404(k) of the Code.[24]

The company stock that an ESOP trust holds must be either (1) common stock that is readily tradable on an established securities market; (2) if no such common stock exists, common stock that has the highest combination of voting power and dividend rights; or (3) preferred stock that is convertible into either of such types of common stock at a reasonable conversion price.[25] Because it is reasonable to pay a higher dividend on preferred stock, a company can increase the amount of dividends it pays if the ESOP trust purchases convertible preferred stock instead of common stock. It also could use a "super-common" class of stock designed to pay a high dividend yield.[26]

An owner of a closely held company who sells convertible preferred stock to an ESOP trust may be precluded from deferring his or her capital gains under Section 1042 of the Code if the preferred stock is characterized by the IRS as "Section 306 stock."[27] One way to avoid this pitfall is to use "super-common" stock instead of preferred stock. If a class of "super-common" stock is created for this purpose, however, any future sales of common stock to the ESOP trust must use such stock because it now will be the class of common stock with the highest combination of voting and dividend rights of any class.

✔ **Inside Loan vs. Outside Loan** In most leveraged ESOP transactions, the ESOP trust does not borrow directly from the lender; rather, the company borrows from the lender and re-loans the proceeds to the ESOP trust (and then, of course, makes yearly contributions to the ESOP trust so the ESOP trust can repay the loan to the company). There is no need for the "inside" loan from the company to the ESOP trust to have the same terms as the "outside" loan from the lender to the company unless the company wants its tax deductions to exactly match its external loan payments.[28] Thus, the company in the example above could obtain a loan from an external lender with a term of 10 years and then make an internal loan to the ESOP trust with a loan term of 24 years, provided that the internal ESOP loan is not using the principal-only release formula (in which case the loan term is limited to 10 years). (With dividend payments as noted above, the ESOP loan could have a shorter term.)

Making an internal ESOP loan with a substantially longer term than the external loan is a fiduciary decision, and the ESOP trustee(s) (or other fiduciary making the decision) must be able to show that the decision was made primarily in the interest of ESOP participants and beneficiaries. If, for example, the ESOP trust delays distributions until the ESOP loan is repaid in the hypothetical 24-year internal loan term, it may be unreasonable to ask ESOP participants to wait that long and take the risk that the company might go bankrupt or otherwise be unable to fund its repurchase obligations many years hence. If the company extends the term of the internal ESOP loan because otherwise there would be no ESOP in the first place (because the Section 404 limits would be exceeded), as in this example, the fiduciaries would have a good argument to agree to such extension. It might be, however, that the ESOP fiduciary would still negotiate for a shorter delay before distributions begin.[29]

Another fiduciary issue is that the interest rate for the "internal" ESOP loan from the company to the ESOP trust should be reasonable, generally being no higher than the interest rate for the "external" loan or a loan that the ESOP trust could have obtained by soliciting proposals from independent third party lenders.

Applying the Rules

The following hypothetical situations illustrate the interplay of the Section 404 deductible contribution limits, the Section 415 annual allocation limits and the strategies and analytical issues described above. In each case, the old (pre-2002) rules are discussed as well as the new rules.

✔ **Example 1: Non-Leveraged ESOP** XYZ Corporation is a C corporation that sponsors a non-leveraged ESOP. The eligible payroll for XYZ Corporation (payroll that can be counted for deduction and limitation purposes under Sections 404 and 415 of the Code, respectively) is $1,000,000. Aggregate 401(k) plan salary reduction contributions are 5% of eligible payroll, or $50,000. The desired XYZ Corporation deductible contribution to ESOP is $150,000 (15% of eligible payroll).

Joe Employee's eligible pay is $50,000. His salary reduction contribution pursuant to the 401(k) plan is $7,500 (15% of eligible pay). Joe Employee's share of the ESOP contribution is $7,500 (15% of eligible pay). His total contribution (401(k) salary reduction contributions plus the ESOP contribution) is $15,000.

For plan years starting before 2002, this set of facts would have caused two problems: First, Joe Employee would receive allocations of 30% of eligible pay (or $15,000) in the form of 401(k) plan salary reduction contributions and ESOP contributions, which would violate the annual addition limits under Section 415 of the Code. Joe Employee would be capped at $12,500 (i.e., 25% of his eligible pay, which was the annual addition limitation under Section 415 of the Code). Second, without a money purchase pension plan feature (i.e., fixed contributions), the deductible contributions to the ESOP would be capped at 15% of eligible payroll, which would be reduced by 401(k) plan salary reduction contributions (5% of eligible payroll in this case).[30] Total contributions pursuant to the 401(k) plan and the ESOP here for all employees would be 20% of eligible payroll (15% ESOP contribution plus 5% 401(k) salary reduction contributions in the aggregate). Therefore, XYZ Corporation would exceed the 15% maximum deductible contribution limits under Section 404(a)(3) of the Code.

For plan years starting before 2002, if XYZ Corporation wanted to maintain its 15% ($150,000) deductible contribution to the ESOP trust, it would not be able to allow individual salary reduction contributions pursuant to the 401(k) plan. If XYZ Corporation was willing to reduce the contributions to the ESOP trust, it would then have to return salary reduction contributions to employees only if they exceeded the Code Section 415 limits of 25% of eligible pay with respect to salary reduction contributions and ESOP contributions.

Now (for plan years starting in 2002 or thereafter), this set of facts no longer creates a problem for XYC Corporation and its employees. Joe Employee will receive allocations well under the new limitations under Section 415 of the Code that allow him to receive the lesser of 100% of eligible pay

($50,000 in his case) or $41,000 to be contributed on his behalf pursuant to the 401(k) plan and under the ESOP. The amount that XYZ Corporation will contribute on Joe Employee's behalf will be $15,000 in this case ($7,500 of salary reduction contributions and $7,500 of ESOP contributions). XYZ Corporation also would be well under the 25% maximum deductible contribution limit under Section 404(a)(3) of the Code without having to rely upon PLR 200436015 (the one allowing for 25% in contributions to repay ESOP loan principal plus 25% to other defined contribution plans). Furthermore, the allowable contribution under the 25% limit also is greater now because XYZ Corporation no longer (for plan years starting in 2002 or thereafter) must reduce 401(k) salary reduction contributions in determining the amount of eligible payroll for purposes of the 25% limit.

✔ **Example 2: Leveraged ESOP for C Corporation** ABC, Inc., is a C corporation that sponsors a leveraged ESOP and also a 401(k) plan. The payroll of eligible employees is $1,000,000 per year. Aggregate salary reduction contributions pursuant to the 401(k) plan are $50,000.

For plan years starting before 2002, ABC, Inc., could contribute to the ESOP trust a maximum of $187,500 as deductible contributions under Code Section 404(a)(9) ($1,000,000 [eligible payroll] minus $50,000 [401(k) plan salary reduction contributions] multiplied by 25% and minus $50,000 [401(k) plan salary reduction contributions]) to repay principal on an ESOP acquisition loan.

For plan years starting in 2002 or thereafter, the deductible contribution limit under Section 404(a)(9) of the Code for ABC, Inc. for purposes of making contributions to repay principal on an ESOP acquisition loan is 25% of eligible payroll or $250,000 (without regard to 401(k) plan salary reduction contributions).

For plan years starting before 2002 *or* in 2002 or thereafter, ABC, Inc., also may make tax-deductible contributions to the ESOP in an amount necessary for the ESOP to repay interest on the loan. These contributions are deductible in addition to the $250,000 limit for principal payments on an

ESOP loan under Section 404(a)(9) of the Code. Interest on an ESOP loan and forfeitures of leveraged ESOP shares of company stock also are not counted for purposes of the limits on annual additions under Section 415 of the Code, provided that not more than one-third of the employer contributions are allocated to the ESOP accounts of "highly compensated employees" (within the meaning of Section 414(q) of the Code). Furthermore, ABC, Inc., may declare and pay reasonable dividends to the ESOP trust (on both allocated and unallocated shares of company stock acquired with the proceeds of an ESOP loan) above and beyond these limits to repay the ESOP's debt. Such dividends are deductible in the taxable year of ABC, Inc., in which they are used for such purposes and are not counted for purposes of the annual addition limits under Section 415 of the Code.

✔ **Example 3: Leveraged ESOP for S Corporation (contrast with Example 2)** EssCo., Inc., an S corporation, sponsors a leveraged ESOP. It maintains a 401(k) plan. The payroll of eligible employees is $1,000,000 per year. Aggregate salary reduction contributions pursuant to the 401(k) plan are $50,000.

For plan years starting before 2002, the deductible contribution limit under Section 404(a)(3) of the Code for purposes of making contributions to repay both principal and interest on an ESOP acquisition loan would have been 15% of eligible payroll (reduced by 401(k) plan salary reduction contributions) less 401(k) plan salary reduction contributions, or $92,500 (($1,000,000 – $50,000) × .15 – $50,000) unless EssCo. has added a money purchase pension plan feature (i.e., a fixed contribution feature) to its ESOP, in which case the deductible contribution that EssCo may make to its ESOP in order to repay both principal and interest on an ESOP acquisition loan would be 25% of eligible payroll or $187,500 (($1,000,000 – $50,000) × .25 – $50,000).[31]

Now (for plan years starting in 2002 and thereafter), the deductible contribution limit under Section 404(a)(3) of the Code for purposes of making contributions to repay both principal and interest on an ESOP acquisition loan is 25% of eligible payroll (including 401(k) plan salary reduction contributions) or $250,000, even if EssCo does not maintain a money purchase pension plan feature as part of its ESOP.

For plan years starting before 2002 *or* in 2002 or thereafter, EssCo may declare and pay distributions of earnings on both allocated and unallocated shares of company stock above and beyond these limits in order to repay the ESOP's debt. Such distributions are not deductible but also are not counted for purposes of the annual addition limits under Section 415 of the Code.

Notes

1. For a more detailed explanation of the contribution and allocation rules themselves, see Luis Granados, "Contribution and Allocation Limits for Leveraged ESOPs," in *Leveraged ESOPs and Employee Buyouts,* 5th ed. (Oakland, CA: NCEO, 2005).

2. For example, it appears that the California Legislature will not make the California franchise tax laws consistent with EGTRRA.

3. Code § 404(a)(3)(A)(i).

4. EGTRRA § 614; Code § 404(n).

5. If a money purchase pension plan is already in place, terminating it raises various issues. A company wishing to discard such a plan because it is no longer necessary should consult with qualified counsel before doing so.

6. EGTRRA § 614; Code § 404(n).

7. See Code § 409(n)(1).

8. Private Letter Ruling (PLR) 9442015.

9. Code § 4972.

10. Before 2002, this was especially true because exceeding the Section 404 limits usually meant exceeding the Section 415 annual addition limits as well, which subjected the ESOP to disqualification. The expanded limits under Section 415 of the Code mean that this is no longer the case; it is now Section 404, not Section 415, that is likely to be the main factor in restricting what a company can contribute to an ESOP trust or other qualified retirement plan trust, provided that a company does not take advantage of the additional room for deductible contributions under PLR 200436015.

11. An eligible individual account plan (EIAP) is a defined contribution plan under Section 407(d)(3)(A) of ERISA that is exempt from ERISA's general diversification rules, i.e., it may invest up to 100% of its assets in qualifying employer securities. An ESOP is an example of an EIAP. For purposes of this discussion (contributing an amount equal to 25% of eligible payroll pursuant to an ESOP and another 25% pur-

suant to a different plan that is an EIAP), the EIAP might be a profit sharing plan, for example.

12. Note, however, that an S corporation may decide to switch to C corporation status (which it might do, for example, so the seller can elect the Section 1042 tax-deferred reinvestment) during its calendar/fiscal year of the year in which the initial ESOP transaction occurs. In this case (assuming the ESOP has already been established while the company was an S corporation), the company may contribute an amount equal to up to 25% of eligible payroll under Code Section 404(a)(3) (i.e., 25% of eligible payroll for the period during which it is an S corporation) that is used to purchase company stock in the ESOP transaction. After the company switches to C status, it can contribute and deduct an amount equal to 25% of eligible payroll (i.e., 25% of the payroll for the part of the year during which it is a C corporation) to repay the principal on the ESOP loan, plus interest and deductible dividends, under Code Sections 404(a)(9) and 404(k), respectively, for the remainder of the year, *plus* an additional 25% of eligible payroll (again, 25% of eligible payroll for the period it is a C corporation) to another defined contribution plan under Code Section 404(a)(3). For example, if the company maintains an ESOP and switches from S to C status midway through the year, the total contribution limit for defined contribution plans will be 25% of the eligible payroll for the first six months (plus potential S corporation distributions for that period used to repay the ESOP loan) plus 50% of eligible payroll for the last six months (plus contributions used to pay interest on the ESOP loan through the tax return filing extension deadline and Code Section 404(k) dividends for the year in question that are used to repay the ESOP loan on or before the end of the year).

13. Code § 404(a)(9)(C) specifically provides that the interest exclusion does not apply to S corporations.

14. Code §§ 404(a)(9) and 415(c)(6). Under Code Section 414(q), highly compensated employees are defined as (1) 5%-or-more owners or (2) those who earned over $90,000 per year in salary during the previous year (as of 2002; this dollar figure is indexed for inflation) and, if the company so elects, were also in the top 20% of employees when ranked on the basis of compensation.

15. Code § 404(k)(5)(A).

16. Code § 4975(f), as amended by the American Jobs Creation Act of 2004. Previously, the IRS had privately ruled that distributions of earnings on allocated shares of company stock could not be used to repay an ESOP trust's loan (see, e.g., PLR 199938052, among others).

17. EGTRRA §§ 632(a)(1) and 611(b) and Code §§ 415(c)(1)(A) and (B).

18. Code § 415(e).

19. Code § 415(c)(6).

20. The restriction of dividends to the repayment of the loan used to acquire the shares of company stock on which such dividends are paid

applies to employer securities acquired by an ESOP after August 4, 1989. Omnibus Budget Reconciliation Act of 1989, P.L. 101-239, § 7302(b) (1989).

21. The IRS finalized its examination guidelines (the "Guidelines") for ESOPs through a supplement (dated November 13, 1996) adding Chapter 500 to the Employee Plans Examination Guidelines Handbook of the Internal Revenue Manual. The Guidelines address certain ESOP qualification requirements under Sections 401(a), 409, and 4975(e)(7) of the Code, as well as requirements for ESOP loans, ESOP dividends, and certain ESOP tax incentives under the Code (including the interest exclusion of Section 133 and tax-deferred sales under Section 1042). On March 11, 1998, the IRS reissued the ESOP examination guidelines with minor revisions (including a reference to the repeal of Code Section 133 by the Small Business Job Protection Act of 1996) as Chapter 4 of the newly reorganized Employee Plans Examination Guidelines Handbook of the Internal Revenue Manual.

22. PLR 9304003.

23. *Steel Balls, Inc. v. Commissioner,* 89 F.3d 841 (8th Cir. 1996). *Steel Balls* was an extreme case in which the ESOP had only one participant but nevertheless reported $589,077 in ESOP dividends in a single year. Although few other companies may find themselves in similar circumstances, the case established a precedent for recharacterizing excess dividends as contributions subject to the Section 415 limits, thus potentially disqualifying the entire plan.

24. PLR 9522041. In this case, the company was publicly traded and the dividend could have amounted to 12%, which at the time, when interest rates were extremely low, was in the high range for publicly traded securities comparable to the security acquired by the ESOP trust.

25. Code § 409(l).

26. Super-common stock is not permitted in some states (e.g., California).

27. When preferred stock received in a plan of recapitalization is then sold to an ESOP in a transaction to which Section 1042 of the Code applies, due diligence should be exercised to ensure that tax deferral is in fact achieved under Section 1042 of the Code. If an individual making such a sale continues to actually or constructively own an equity interest in the company following the sale, the preferred stock received pursuant to the plan of recapitalization and then sold to the ESOT may constitute stock described in Section 306 of the Code because (1) it is stock, other than common stock, which was distributed to the shareholder pursuant to a plan of reorganization in which the shareholder did not recognize a gain, and (2) the effect of the individual's receipt of preferred stock in the plan of recapitalization may be substantially the same as the receipt of a stock dividend due to the equity interest which the individual continues to hold. Preferred stock may be able to avoid the taint of Section 306 if it is struc-

tured so that the preferred stock has features similar to common stock (except for the dividend). Section 302 also includes certain other exceptions to dividend treatment.

28. The only exception would be if the loan from the lender was made under Section 133 of the Code, which allowed commercial lenders to exclude from their taxable income 50% of the interest income from ESOP loans meeting certain requirements. In such cases, the loan from the company to the ESOP trust had to be on substantially similar terms as the loan from the bank to the company. Congress repealed Section 133 of the Code by Section 1602 of the Small Business Jobs Protection Act of 1996 for loans incurred after August 20, 1996, except for loans for which a binding written commitment was in effect by June 9, 1996.

29. Companies that want to extend the internal ESOP loan for other reasons have a harder argument. If, for example, a company wants to arrange a 7-year term loan from an external lender and then turn around and lend the proceeds to the ESOP trust on a 20-year term loan simply so that it can decrease the yearly contributions it makes to the ESOP trust for the participants, this might be questionable. Some companies extend the term of the internal ESOP loan, however, so that they can "smooth out" contributions over a long term, which can have the positive effect of letting the company to still be able to provide contributions for new employees who become employed some years after the ESOP has been put in place. This would be more justifiable than an internal ESOP loan term that was extended just for the company's financial convenience.

30. Please refer, however, to the planning technique under Sections 404(a)(3) and 404(a)(9) of the Code as described in PLR 200436015 and PLR 9548036.

31. Id.

7

S Corporations and ESOPs

Corey Rosen

Until 1998, the issue of how to deal with ESOPs in S corporations was simple: S corporations could not have ESOPs. But effective January 1 of that year, that rule was changed, and in 1999, things got even better. ESOPs would not have to pay federal (and often state) income tax on their share of the profits in an S corporation. Still, with capital gains rates at 28% federally, and with many states adding their own taxes, almost all owners of S corporations wanting to sell to an ESOP converted to C status first, perhaps with the intention of eventually (after at least the required five years) switching back to S to take advantage of the special ESOP S corporation tax benefits. That decision has become more complicated now that federal capital gains taxes are only 15%. While most S corporation business owners still find it worthwhile to convert to C first, some choose to stay S. On the other hand, once the sale is made, it is increasingly the case that ESOPs buy the remaining shares as soon as possible and become 100% S corporations, paying no federal, and often no state, income taxes.

This chapter looks at the issues involved in selling to an ESOP in an S corporation and, more briefly, converting to S status after the sale. For those interested in more details on this topic, the NCEO publishes a book specifically on the topic of S corporation ESOPs.

How S Corporation and C Corporation ESOP Rules Differ

S corporations are taxed like partnerships. That is, corporate profits are passed directly through to the owners; the corporation does not pay tax. Thanks to legislation effective January 1, 1998, ESOPs (and only ESOPs) are exempted from the requirement that nontaxable entities pay unrelated business income tax (UBIT) on any profit attributed to their ownership share. The theory was that when employees leave the plan, gains the profits have helped build into their stock value will be taxed, almost always at ordinary income tax rates. So to tax them earlier would be double taxation, violating a basic S corporation principle.

Although this is a substantial tax benefit, S corporation ESOPs also have some tax disadvantages:

- Sellers to ESOPs in S corporations cannot take advantage of the tax-deferred "rollover" under Section 1042 of the Internal Revenue Code (the "Code"), which allows sellers to ESOPs in C corporations to indefinitely defer taxation on the gains from the sale if the ESOP holds 30% or more of the company after the sale.

- S corporation ESOPs cannot deduct dividends (i.e., S corporation distributions) paid on ESOP shares.

- Interest payments on an ESOP loan in S corporation ESOPs count toward the contribution limits.

- It also appears that if distributions are passed directly through to participants in an S corporation ESOP, they are not deductible to the company, as passed-through dividends are in C corporation ESOPs. This issue was not specially addressed by the legislation, however, so there is still some uncertainty about it.

Weighing the Pros and Cons of Converting to C Status First

As noted above, most sellers to an ESOP in an S corporation convert to C status first and then complete the sale (which can be done as soon as the next day). Under S corporation rules, when companies convert from S to C status, they cannot reconvert back to S status until five years have elapsed.

The most obvious issue in making the S-to-C decision is whether the Section 1042 tax deferral is worthwhile. There are a number of pros and cons here.

✔ **Arguments for Converting** Although capital gains rates are lower than they once were, even just a 15% deferral may be a significant benefit. For instance, assume a seller sells for $3 million, all of it gain. With the deferral, $450,000 can be deferred. If the seller holds onto replacement investments for seven years, and the investments are in a diversified equity portfolio, that $450,000 will, given historic rates of return, yield an additional $450,000 in gain. A portfolio with more bonds in it would take longer to double the $450,000. This calculation, however, does not assess the impact of inflation, which would make the present value of the $450,000 less in today's dollars. It is also does not look at the differential investment return scenarios provided by the ability to invest in any kind of investment if deferral is not chosen, or how those different strategies would be affected by future taxation. Still, however it is calculated, the deferral is a significant opportunity for most business owners.

Second, for most sellers, the 15% capital gains rate is only part of the story. State taxes can often add a few to several additional percentage points, and sellers who are subject to the alternative minimum tax, or AMT (a common occurrence for higher-income taxpayers, especially in high-tax states) may find that if they do not choose to defer the gain, they can end up with an AMT penalty on the capital gains tax they pay of a few percent or more. That's primarily because capital gains reduce the AMT exemption by one dollar for every four dollars in gain. The reasoning behind this is complicated, but the bottom line is that without deferral, the AMT might be as much as $20,000 or so more than it would otherwise be. The tax issues, in short, are more complicated than "15% or deferral." Sellers should consult a qualified accountant and get a specific estimate of just what the tax effects will be.

Third, C corporation ESOPs are more flexible. In an S corporation, there can only be one class of shares. In a C corporation, there can be multiple classes. It is common in C corporation ESOPs, for instance, for the ESOP to own convertible preferred stock (the ESOP can own these shares if they are convertible at the discretion of the trustee into voting common shares) or super-common shares (shares with additional dividend or possibly voting rights). Other owners, meanwhile, have regular common shares. This allows the company to issue a dividend just to the ESOP, usually to help repay an ESOP loan. Because of the special nature of these shares, the dividend rate can be higher than with common stock, while the stock's underlying value will go up and down less than with conventional common stock. These special features may also be used to make a stronger case that an ESOP that buys a non-controlling interest in the first of a series of planned transactions can pay a control price throughout these transaction. S corporations, in contrast, can only have one class of stock.

Fourth, there are potential problems when there are other owners and the ESOP in an S corporation buys less than 100% of the stock. Because S corporations can have only one class of shares, if there are distributions to the other owners (most commonly so they can pay their taxes on their share of corporate earnings), a pro-rata distribution must be made to the ESOP. If this were not done, the ESOP would be deemed to own a second class of stock. So if the company earns $1 million, and a 30% distribution is made to the 70% owners, the ESOP gets 30% as well. The 70% owners would get $210,000 of the distribution, and the ESOP would get $90,000. The ESOP's portion would be allocated to employee accounts, where it can be used to buy additional shares, repurchase shares from departing participants, or to provide diversification, but the distribution to the ESOP may be more than what the remaining owners are comfortable with. This becomes especially problematic when the ESOP owns a large percentage of the shares.

Finally, the contribution and deduction limits for C and S corporation ESOPs are different. In either case, companies can deduct up to 25% of eligible compensation for straight cash or stock contributions to the ESOP, but the rules for leveraged ESOPs are different. In a C corporation, up to 25% of covered compensation can be used to repay the principal on an ESOP loan. Interest payments are disregarded for this purpose. Dividends are deductible (and are not included in the 25% limit). And the IRS has confirmed in Private Letter Ruling 200436015 that the 25% limit for contributions to repay the principal on an ESOP loan is separate from and in addition to the 25% limit for other defined contribution plans. In S corporations, interest payments count toward the 25% limit. Distributions of earnings are not deductible (but they, like C corporation dividends, are not included in the 25% limit). And the 25% limit covers both contributions for repaying ESOP loan principal and contributions to other defined contribution plans, so contributions to other plans (like a qualified profit sharing plan) reduce what can be contributed to a leveraged ESOP. Where payroll is small relative to the value of the shares sold, these limits may make the acquisition less practical in an S corporation scenario. One way to deal with this problem, however, is to repay the loan to the ESOP over a longer period of time than the loan to the outside lender (typically, there is a loan to the company that is reloaned to the ESOP, but the two loans do not have to be on the same terms). The longer term on the ESOP loan will spread contributions out more so they stay within contribution limits, but it also means that the deductions on the ESOP loan are being taken more slowly than the outside loan is being repaid.

✔ **Arguments Against Converting**   While the advantages of the Section 1042 tax deferral are very attractive, there are also good arguments for not converting to C status:

- *Corporate-level taxation:* As a C corporation, profits are taxed at the corporate level and, ultimately, taxed again at the owner level. For many leveraged ESOPs, this is not much of an issue because even as a C corporation, the contributions the company makes to repay the ESOP loan may wipe out much of the corporate-level tax anyway, and once the loan is repaid, the company generally can convert to S status. But this is not true for every ESOP. If there are significant corporate-level taxes left over, it is worth evaluating how significant the tax impact will be. If there are significant corporate-level earnings after the sale, even with the ESOP contributions, the tax shelter offered by the ESOP may be an attractive consideration. If the ESOP owns 30% of the stock, for instance, 30% of these profits are not taxable. This tax shield may give the company the ability to grow faster, thus enhancing the share value of the remaining non-ESOP owners.

- *Issues with other owners:* A similar consideration is if there are other owners not selling to the ESOP. For instance, say Mary owns 30% of the company and sells all her stock to the ESOP. John and Phil do not sell, although they may do so later. While Mary benefits from the conversion to C status by being able to roll over her gains in a tax-deferred manner under Section 1042, the other owners now find that their earnings that would have been sheltered from the corporate-level tax no longer are. If the sale does not create enough deductions to reduce the corporate-level tax low enough to satisfy these owners, they may not want to convert. A possible solution to this if converting to C status is to pay out earnings to the other owners in the form of additional compensation, which is, of course, deductible. This compensation must be reasonable, however, and this approach won't work for non-employee owners.

  Also, as noted above, if there are distributions to non-ESOP owners (most commonly so they can pay their taxes on their share of corporate earnings), a pro-rata distribution must be made to the ESOP (because S corporations can have only a single class of stock). These distributions to the ESOP may be more than what the remaining owners are comfortable with, especially where the ESOP owns a larger percentage of the shares.

- *Large amounts of undistributed earnings (the accumulated adjustments account):* Some S corporations have significant undistributed earnings that the company may not have retained in cash. When the conversion to C status takes place, any earnings that have not yet been contributed to the owners must be distributed in one year or they are taxable to the owners (meaning they will be taxed twice, since the owners have already paid tax on them before). If the company does not have the cash to do this, it could borrow money, but the ESOP may itself require too much cash to make this payout practical.

- *Asset sales:* Another potential drawback to conversion is if the ESOP buys less than 100% of the stock, and sellers ultimately plan to sell the company in an asset sale. In an S corporation, the sale of the company's assets trigger only a single tax at the individual level; in a C corporation, the sale would be taxed at both the corporate and individual level, as income to the company and as capital gains to the individuals. The amount of the corporate tax would depend in part on the depreciation taken on the assets.

  Even if the sale of the C corporation is a stock sale, it could still be taxed as an asset sale. If the purchaser makes an election under Section 338 of the Code to treat the sale as an asset sale, the basis of the acquired assets can be stepped up to the price paid for the stock. This would allow greater amortization and depreciation deductions for the purchaser in the future. On the other hand, the acquired corporation will be treated as if it had sold its assets. The purchaser then bears the tax on the constructive gain recognized by the selling company. For these reasons, as well as a desire to avoid any liabilities the company may face that attach to the sale of shares (such as outstanding lawsuits), purchasers prefer asset sales.

- *Loss flow-through:* A less common consideration is if the S corporation is creating losses the owners want flowed through to them. In some situations, a company may be making heavy investments, often in real property or other hard assets, that create paper losses. These losses can be flowed through to the owners, who can deduct them at a marginally higher rate than can the company. In some scenarios, this may be desirable.

- *High basis:* It is not unusual in an S corporation for the owner to have a relatively high basis in the stock, often because the owner's basis has been adjusted upward by the company retaining earnings rather than distributing them out. In that case, there is little benefit to the rollover.

- *Relatives and 25% owners:* As described in detail elsewhere in this book, when a seller elects the tax-deferral opportunity in an ESOP sale under Section 1042 of the Code, sellers to the ESOP, more-than-25% owners and their direct relatives, and the lineal ascendants, descendants, spouses, and siblings of the seller cannot receive an allocation of the stock subject to the rollover for at least 10 years. If the seller wants to include these people in the ESOP, then retaining S corporation status may make sense. However, if these people constitute a significant percentage of payroll, they may not be able to receive allocations under the S corporation "anti-abuse" rules described below.

- *Restrictions on qualified replacement property are not acceptable:* Despite the tremendous tax advantages of the rollover, some sellers strongly prefer to invest in mutual funds, government bonds, or other investments that do not qualify as "qualified replacement property" under Section 1042, in which case there is no reason to convert to C status first.

Conversion Issues from S to C

Conversion from an S to a C corporation must occur within 2½ months of the end of the fiscal year. If a company uses LIFO (last in, first out) accounting procedures, there is an immediate recapture over four years of any excess inventory (not assets) with LIFO over what would have been the case with FIFO (first in, first out). As noted above, care must taken to manage distribution taxes on the accumulated adjustments account in ways that are acceptable to the owners. Conversion back to S status cannot occur for five years after conversion to C status.

✔ **Anti-Abuse Rules in S Corporations**   If a company decides to stay S rather than convert (or later converts back to S), particular care must be taken to avoid the S corporation anti-abuse rules. These were created in 2001 to address the misuse of S corporations ESOPs to benefit just one or a few usually highly paid individuals. In a few cases (but only a few), the rules can trap some legitimate ESOPs as well. The anti-abuse rules work through a series of tests described below:

First, define "disqualified persons." Under the law, a "disqualified person" is an individual who owns 10% or more of the allocated and unallocated shares in the ESOP or who, together with family members (spouses or other family members, including lineal ancestors or descendants, siblings and their children, or the spouses of any of these other family members) owns 20% or more. Synthetic equity, broadly defined to include stock options, stock appreciation rights, and other equity equivalents, is also counted as ownership (in effect, ownership in the ESOP) for this determination.

Second, determine whether disqualified individuals own at least 50% of all shares in the company. In making this determination, ownership is defined to include shares held directly, shares owned through synthetic equity, and allocated or unallocated shares owned through the ESOP.

Synthetic equity is very broadly defined for this purpose. It includes not only stock options, stock appreciation rights, phantom stock, and similar equity equivalent or equity-based bonus plans, but also any other deferred rights (rights payable after more than 2.5 years) that would draw down a company's earnings, apparently including life insurance, deferred cash compensation arrangements, or rights to a share of future earnings. Companies must calculate the present value of these future benefits and translate them into a share equivalent. This does not mean that companies cannot have these plans; it does mean that such deferred compensation has to be within what for most companies will be reasonable limits. The regulations on this issue were created because some promoters of ersatz ESOPs saw such deferred compensation plans as ways to channel most of the company's benefits to a few highly paid individuals in away that avoided any corporate tax.

If disqualified individuals own at least 50% of the stock of the company, then these individuals may not receive an allocation from the ESOP during that year without a substantial tax penalty. If such an allocation does occur, it is taxed as a distribution to the recipient, and a 50% corporate excise tax would apply to the fair market value of the stock allocated. If synthetic equity is owned, a 50% excise tax would also apply to its value as well. In the first year in which this rule applies, there is a 50% tax on the fair market value of shares allocated to disqualified individuals even if no additional allocations are made to those individuals that year (in other words, the tax applies simply if disqualified individuals own more than 50% of the company in the first year).

For plans in existence before March 14, 2001, the rules become effective for plan years beginning after December 31, 2004. For plans established after March 14, 2001, or for preexisting C corporation ESOPs that switched to S status after this date, the effective date is for plan years ending after March 14, 2001.

In addition, the conference report on the bill directed the IRS to develop regulations to define existing plans as subject to this legislation, regardless of when they were established, if their purpose is "in substance, an avoidance or evasion of the prohibited allocation rule." The IRS has acted aggressively on this ability.

These regulations are complicated; they are described in more detail in our book on S corporation ESOPs. Essentially, however they block three kinds of common abuses. The first is where a management company is set up as a 100% ESOP-owned S corporation, with a separate operating company functioning as a C corporation. The C corporation may or may not have an ESOP, but the management company charges most of the company's profits as earnings, which flow back to the management company where they are not taxed (because the company is 100% ESOP-owned). Another scam uses various kinds of deferred compensation arrangements (stock options, insurance, rabbi trusts, etc.) to provide management with equity equivalents that are designed to get around the S anti-abuse rules. The third sets up a series of S corporation subsidiaries, often owned by one person through some kind of synthetic stock (options, phantom stock, and similar plans), with profits effectively shielded by being allocated to the subsidiaries.

In each of these scenarios, the IRS has ruled that these approaches violate the anti-abuse rules and are subject to the draconian tax consequences described above. In addition, the plans may be disqualified, causing even further tax pain. Conventional S corporation ESOPs have little, if any problem, with any of these rules. At most, they simply require more administrative monitoring. Some very small ESOP companies (typically under 10 or 15 employees) may find the rules make it impractical, however, to have an ESOP because of the distribution of ownership in the plan.

Conclusion

There is no right or wrong answer to whether to convert before selling to an ESOP. Unfortunately, there is usually not a simple answer either. Owners should consult with qualified professional advisors to compare different scenarios, looking at taxes, investments, plan structure, and other issues. The good news is that either way, a sale to an ESOP can provide substantial tax benefits to the seller, the employees, and the company.

CHAPTER 8

CASE STUDIES OF CLOSELY HELD ESOP COMPANIES

LeFiell Manufacturing

COREY ROSEN

Few companies do more to create an ownership culture, or have done it longer, than LeFiell Manufacturing, a 200-employee manufacturer of tubular components for commercial aircraft and the space industry (LeFiell hardware has been used in the Space Shuttle). Started in 1930, the Santa Fe Springs, CA, company began its ESOP in 1974, just after the law authorizing ESOPs, the Employee Retirement Income Security Act (ERISA), was passed. The ESOP was started mostly as an employee benefit. New shares were printed each year and the company took a corresponding tax deduction—and the owners took the dilution. That continued until 1986, when the ESOP owned 30.5% of the shares. From that point on, the company contributed cash to the ESOP to buy shares from existing owners.

Today, the ESOP owns 65% of the stock, 25% is owned by current employees, and 10% is owned by retired and terminated employees. When C.K. LeFiell, the original owner, died, he willed his remaining 30% ownership to individual employees and members of the board.

✔ **ESOP Structure** The company's board of directors consists of seven employees from all areas of the company plus a corporate lawyer and one retired employee. Five of the board members are elected to the ESOP Committee, which deals with plan policy and administration. A five-member ESOP advisory committee consists of self-nominated employees who serve as the main communications and ESOP culture vehicle for the company. Employees on the committee must get outside training, including attending ESOP conferences and seminars. An ESOP newsletter helps keep people informed about developments in the plan and the company.

✔ **Getting Employees Involved**   Like most successful ESOP companies, LeFiell has a lot of meetings. For instance, the town hall meeting is a monthly lunch the company buys for any employee on any of the three shifts who wants to attend. George Ray, LeFiell's president, hosts the meetings, including the 2:15 a.m. lunch for the third shift. At first, not that many people came, but now attendance is high, and near perfect on the second and third shifts. The meetings provide a chance for employees to raise any issues of concern to them and for Ray to discuss company developments. There is also an semiannual recognition dinner for outstanding employee performance and service, plus "ice cream days" to celebrate successes and open houses where spouses and family can come to visit the plant.

The company shares financial and performance information with employees at the corporate and work unit level. These numbers can be used as the basis for ad-hoc teams to address specific problems. For instance, last year, management decided they need to improve their on-time delivery, which had stood at 65%. Employees were challenged to bring it to 90%. In three months, they figured out how to do it. Management then cooked them hamburgers on all three shifts.

As these examples illustrate, a persistent theme in the meetings is having fun. Companies always need to connect fun activities to an ESOP theme, Ray says, showing how prosperity can be created through ownership responsibility.

One of the ways the company shares financial information is in a "Personal Statement of Benefits and Compensation" it gives to all employees. The statement makes it clear just how much more the company pays to have an employee than is reflected in wages.

✔ **Sharing Success**   Starting in 1994, LeFiell began to pay annual dividends to ESOP participants. Ray says it is one of the best things the company has done. Not only does it provide an immediate benefit for employees, but it creates a reason to talk about how the company is doing—and how it might do better. The dividend amounts have been substantial. In 2000, the company paid out $638,000 in dividends to the 330 people in the plan (i.e., current workers and former employees not yet paid out). The average dividend check in 1999 for an employee with less than three years' service was only $22, but for the most senior employees it was $11,796. While new employees may not get much, they can see that if they stay, the dividend checks will be substantial.

The company pays people out in installments over five years, during which time their account balances remain in company stock. Ray says that they do this because they want to reward former employees—and give them a reason to care about leaving the company in good shape. That includes making sure that someone can take over your job when you leave. Given the good years LeFiell had in the 1990s, that has meant a windfall for departed employees. Ray gives the example of an employee whose account started at $209,080 in 1996, paid out $190,000 in dividends and redemptions over the next three years, and left the employee with a balance to be paid of $141,215.

Ray notes that the company has participated in the general good times that have benefited much of the U.S. economy. Slower growth in the future is a possibility that he and others at LeFiell are careful to communicate to employees. But the company's long-term commitment to employee ownership is expected to continue to reap dividends for a long time to come.

ComSonics, Inc.

Ronald J. Gilbert

ComSonics, Inc., of Harrisonburg, VA, is a 100% ESOP-owned S corporation. The ESOP was established 27 years ago and gradually acquired stock in the company until the ESOP became a 100% owner. ComSonics employs approximately 150 employees and is a major manufacturer and repairer of cable television leakage detection quipment. ComSonics is an innovator in this field, holding many patents, and the equipment is sold throughout the world. The company motto is "We set the standards."

Six steps, outlined below, are being pursued by ComSonics to increase the value of the company for its employee shareholders. Simultaneously, however, the board of directors of ComSonics, on which I serve, believes that these steps also substantially increase the probability that ComSonics will remain employee owned. The steps are:

1. Employee involvement

2. Voting pass-through

3. Conversion to S corporation status

4. Stock buyback

5. Subsidiaries

6. Acquisitions

✔ **Employee Involvement and Education**   From the inception of the ESOP, it was recognized by Warren Braun, ComSonics's founder and chairman emeritus, that employee involvement and education was essential in order to maximize the potential of the ESOP. Over the years, various strategies have been used to implement this objective. A professor from the local college was brought in at one time to teach a course on basic finance. The long-term and most successful strategy has been the establishment of an ESOP committee. One of the principal functions of the ESOP committee is to educate all employees on a continuing basis regarding the ESOP. Members of the ESOP committee are non-management and are elected from different functional areas of the company. They elect their chair, who automatically becomes a voting member of the ComSonic's board of directors.

Financial and performance information is shared freely with the employee-owners, providing them with constant measurement criteria regarding the performance of the company and its varying functional areas.

✔ **Voting Pass-Through** A second strategy implemented in 1989 is the full voting pass-through for all vested shares. Therefore, in addition to having the right to vote their allocated shares for the seven "voting pass-through" issues required by the Internal Revenue Code, ComSonics' employees vote their vested allocated shares for the election of the board of directors. The ComSonics board currently consists of nine members, four of whom are outside directors.

✔ **S Corporation Status** In August 1998, ComSonics elected S corporation status. ESOPs in S corporations do not have to pay income taxes on their share of corporate earnings. This has been a major factor in assisting the company to meet its current and projected ESOP repurchase obligation. Funds that would otherwise go to federal or state taxes are being allocated for the repurchase of shares from employees entitled to an ESOP distribution for death, disability, retirement, or "other" terminations. The board of directors recently authorized an accelerated repurchase of the shares in accounts of former employees, largely made possible by the S corporation status that ComSonics now enjoys and the resultant additional earnings that the company has been able to retain.

All former employees are being offered the opportunity to cash out stock currently held in their ESOP accounts. The company expects that the vast majority of participants who are offered this election will accept it. As a result, ComSonics will have fully met its current repurchase liability obligations. Careful planning for the repurchase obligation will still be necessary, but repurchasing the vast majority of existing shares in the accounts of former employees addresses a substantial liability that would have otherwise been addressed over the next five years.

✔ **In-Service Distributions**   Another uncommon feature of the ComSonics ESOP is an "in-service" distribution option. This option is being considered by more companies as the pressure to "take the money and run" increases as ESOP account balances grow. A ComSonics employee with seven years or more of service has the option to take an early partial distribution equal to 20% of his or her current ESOP account balance. Once such an option is elected, the employee is not eligible to exercise the option again for an additional seven years. Of course, the Internal Revenue Code-mandated ESOP diversification election, which begins at age 55 with ten years of service, overrides this early partial distribution option.

✔ **Subsidiaries**   ComSonics has established a number of operating subsidiaries. All but one are functionally identical to operations performed at the parent company level, but formed for geographic purposes. The remaining subsidiary, however, is in an emerging technology area that has substantial potential in a market area that is very poorly defined at this juncture. This subsidiary, should this market develop, would anticipate attracting investment capital from outside sources to share the risk of this emerging technology. It is anticipated that the investors would be interested in equity ownership in the emerging technology subsidiary only, and thus the subsidiary corporate structure was chosen. Thus, ComSonics, Inc., at the holding company level, would remain 100% employee owned, while it is possible that in the future, at least one of the subsidiary companies would have substantial ownership by non-employees.

✔ **Acquisitions**   As a profitable company that seeks to grow shareholder value, ComSonics is pursuing an acquisition strategy directly related to its core competencies, as well as in other related areas. The principal objective of this acquisition strategy is to increase shareholder value, in part by leveraging the company's outstanding reputation in the cable TV industry, as well as to take advantage of a management structure positioned to manage profitably a company with a substantially larger revenue base. It is also recognized that only through an acquisition strategy would the company have the opportunity to go public. Thus, the acquisition strategy, while not motivated by the desire to be a publicly traded company, recognizes that for this particular company in this particular industry, only an acquisition strategy might make an IPO a viable option. Of course, becoming publicly traded in an active market means that an ESOP company's repurchase obligation essentially disappears. Employees who become eligible for distributions from the ESOP would be free to hold the shares or sell them whenever they please in the public marketplace.

✔ **Summary**   ComSonics, Inc., a 27-year old ESOP that is now 100% owned by the ESOP and operating as an S corporation, has employed, and continues to employ, a number of strategies to enhance shareholder value. These strategies at the same time increase the probability that the company will remain employee owned. Ultimately, if the company were to become publicly traded, the ESOP repurchase obligation would no longer be a factor that might require partial or complete sale of the company.

Haywood Builders Supply

COREY ROSEN

At 7 p.m. on Friday, January 10, 1997, Philip Dooly, president of Haywood Builders Supply in Waynesville, NC, left work. An hour later a raging fire broke out. Three of the company's ten buildings were destroyed, including the main store. The company's records, retail center, offices, and one-third of its inventory were lost. Late Friday night, the company management got employees together and told them "we will be open on Monday." It wasn't really an order; it was a reassurance that the company was going to keep paying its people and give them work to do.

On Saturday morning, most of Haywood's key customers (contractors and home builders) showed up at the site, brought their own tools (because Haywood no longer had any) and worked throughout the day to build a temporary showroom and office space in one of the other buildings on the premises. This was all completely voluntary. On Sunday, friends and local businesses donated desks, paper, and office equipment. Monday morning, Haywood was operational.

The decision to reopen was not an easy one. Some of the family members who still owned part of the business wanted to liquidate. But Haywood was majority owned by an ESOP, and shutting down was not what employee ownership was all about. The decision to stay open apparently was a good one. Two months later, the company had its best sales month ever. In 1998, sales at Haywood exceeded $10 million the first time ever, and in 1999, the company was named the PRO Dealer of the Year (PRO is a hardware dealer group).

All this support came despite the fact that Haywood faces heavy competition from Lowe's and Home Depot (companies whose employees are also owners, although of minority interests in the companies). The Blue Ridge mountain area Waynesville calls home has attracted a growing number of well-off retirees, many of whom are interested in home improvement. The expanding population has attracted the "big box" retailers that can put smaller companies out of business. But, like employee-owned Jackson's Hardware in San Rafael, CA, which faces three big-box dealers within a mile of its store, Haywood has relied on exceptional customer service to stay more than competitive.

✔ **Starting the ESOP**   Haywood Builders Supply was started in 1948 by Philip Dooly's father as a retail outlet for his lumber manufacturing company. When the father died in 1973, leaving eight siblings, a second wife, and a child from that marriage, it created a sticky ownership situation. Dooly took over as President in 1973, but other family members could not agree on the future direction of the company. Although these family members did not want the responsibility of running the business, they did want a say in what was done with it.

The business was nearly sold as a result of the owners' desire for liquidity. At one point a letter of intent was signed and the process of purchase was under way, but the buyer started raising unacceptable conditions and the family killed the deal. After many years of family disputes, Dooly proposed using an ESOP to create some liquidity for the other family members. They investigated the idea, were attracted to the 1042 provision, and began with the process of valuation.

In 1993, a valuation was completed that came in about six percent under what the board of directors had wanted. The ability to defer taxes persuaded them to accept the ESOP's offer, however, and 35% of the company was sold to the plan. Later, this would increase to 70%. Part of the proceeds for the first purchase came out of an long-standing profit sharing plan (but only a minority of plan assets were used); the rest came from a loan. Family members came together to defer their dividends on their remaining shares to help the company repay the loan.

✔ **ESOP Plan Structure and Results**　The plan has a five-year graded vesting schedule. The ESOP generally buys back the shares from departing employees and reallocates them. A corporate owned life insurance policy procedure is in place as one tool for handling repurchase. The plan is trusteed by a corporate officer.

At least initially, the plan's impact was not as great as hoped. Haywood had a long history of profit sharing and generous benefits, so employees already felt well taken care of and loyal to the company. Newer employees, however, have latched on to the idea of employee ownership. Employee interest increased significantly after the company passed through dividends in 1998 and 1999. The company has become identified in the community as being employee owned and that has both helped reinforce employee interest and community support, especially after a big paper mill in the area, Blue Ridge Paper, was bought by employees.

Given the strong competition, the company's 40 employees have had to make some exceptional efforts to keep customers, especially the general contractors who are critical to the success of local hardware suppliers. The company matches any special services offered by competitors, but also takes contractors on outings and works hard to develop special expertise contractors can count on. As individual customers become more important, the company is adding installed sales on various home improvement services. So far, these strategies seem to be paying off.

PART 2

SECTION 1042 AND THE ESOP ROLLOVER

9

AN INTRODUCTION TO SECTION 1042

ROBERT F. SCHATZ

Not infrequently, a significant portion of the wealth of an owner of a successful closely held corporation consists of the stock of his or her corporation, which, while valuable, may not be readily marketable. Often, however, such owners need or desire current liquidity (whether to diversify their current investments, invest in new business opportunities, or fund their retirement or phased withdrawal from the day-to-day operations of the corporation) or future liquidity (to fund, for example, following death, their estates' payment of taxes or other obligations or the continued care and support of their families), and therefore will consider selling all or a portion of their corporate stock.

Section 1042 of the Internal Revenue Code of 1986, as amended (the "Code"), was adopted as a way to encourage employee ownership by giving shareholders a significant tax incentive. If shareholders sell their corporate stock to an employee stock ownership trust (ESOT) established pursuant to an ESOP under the conditions specified in Section 1042 and reinvest the sale proceeds in certain other securities, the selling shareholders may elect to defer paying tax on the gain realized from the sale of their corporate stock until the sale or other disposition of the securities purchased with the sale proceeds. This chapter will focus on the requirements that must be satisfied for the selling shareholder to qualify for this favorable tax treatment.

General Rule

Section 1042 of the Code permits a non-corporate share-holder of a closely held corporation (i.e., a corporation none of the stock of which is, or was within one year before the sale, readily tradable on an established securities market) to elect to defer the recognition of gain that would be recognized as long-term capital gain realized from the sale of his or her employer securities to an ESOT if:

- The corporation is a C corporation (not an S corporation);
- The securities sold to the ESOT constitute "qualifying securities";
- The selling shareholder held the qualifying securities for at least three years;
- After the transaction, the ESOP holds at least 30% of the corporation's stock;
- The selling shareholder files with his or her next tax return, before the due date thereof (including extensions), an election to treat the sale of securities as a sale of qualified securities under Section 1042 and a verified written statement of the company consenting to the imposition, under certain conditions, of a 10% additional tax if the qualified securities are disposed of by the ESOP within three years (see "The Procedural Requirements for Tax Deferral" below); and
- Within three months before or one year after the transaction, the selling shareholder reinvests the sale proceeds in securities of certain other U.S. companies and affirmatively elects at the time of purchase to treat the securities as "qualified replacement property."[1]

However, strict compliance with the requirements set forth below is necessary to qualify for the tax deferral (hereinafter the "1042 tax deferral").

Sale of Qualified Securities to the ESOP

✔ **What Stock May Be Sold in the Transaction** As noted above, only shareholders of closely held corporations can elect the 1042 tax deferral, because the only securities that can constitute "qualified securities" are employer securities that are not readily tradable on an established securities market.[2]

Employer securities, however, may *not* include shares of stock acquired by the selling shareholder (1) as a result of a distribution from a pension, profit sharing plan, or stock bonus plan; (2) pursuant to an option or other right granted (pursuant to a qualified stock option plan) by or on behalf of the corporation whose stock is being sold (or any of its subsidiaries); or (3) in connection with the performance of services. Hence, the 1042 tax deferral would not be available to a shareholder who received his or her shares of employer securities as a result of one of these transactions.[3]

Three-Year Holding Requirement for the Selling Shareholder. The qualified securities sold by the selling shareholder must have been held by the shareholder for a period of not less than three years, determined as of the time of the sale.[4] The three-year period is measured from the time the selling shareholder acquired, or is deemed to have acquired, the qualified securities.

Tacking. The shareholder may carry over ("tack") periods of time that the stock was held by another person from whom the shareholder acquired the qualified securities if, in general, the qualified securities, for purposes of determining gain or loss from a sale or exchange of property, had the same basis in the hands of the selling shareholder as they would have had in the hands of the person from whom the selling shareholder acquired the securities.[5] While a discussion of the tacking rules is beyond the scope of this chapter, examples of permitted tacking of holding periods would include (1) gifts of qualified securities (the recipient of the gifted stock could count the period of time the qualified securities were held by the donor);[6] (2) like-kind exchanges of stock (i.e., the selling shareholder received common stock in exchange for common stock, or preferred stock in exchange for preferred stock);[7] and (3) transactions that qualify as mergers or other tax-free reorganiza-

tions, and which otherwise comply with the specific requirements of the Code applicable to such tax-free reorganizations.[8]

✔ **The 30% Requirement** The ESOP must hold 30% of each
class of stock or 30% of the value of all the corporation's
capital stock as a result of the transaction. However, if there
are multiple selling shareholders and the sales are made in
a single transaction or as part of a single, integrated transaction that results in not less than 30% of the total value of
all outstanding stock of the corporation being owned by the
ESOT immediately after the sale, each of the selling shareholders will be eligible for the 1042 tax deferral. Thus, whenever possible, selling shareholders should coordinate the
sale transaction to occur at a single closing unless the 30%
requirement has already been met.[9]

✔ **ESOP Participation by Selling Shareholders** One of the disadvantages of electing the 1042 tax deferral is the inability
of the selling shareholders, and the effective inability of their
family members, to participate in the ESOP. This prohibition
exists for ten years after the sale or until the indebtedness
incurred to purchase the qualified securities is repaid and
the employer securities purchased from the selling shareholder are fully allocated, whichever is later.[10] However, not
only is the selling shareholder precluded from participating
but also (1) his or her spouse, brothers and sisters, lineal
ancestors, and lineal descendants (unless the lineal descendants as a group receive 5% or less of the employer securities acquired by the ESOT from related persons);[11] and (2)
any other person who owns more than 25% of the value of
the corporation's stock (or 25% of any class thereof).[12] Conversely, if the selling shareholders do not elect the 1042 tax
deferral, then none of this applies.

When determining whether a shareholder owns over 25%
of the corporation's stock, stock owned directly or indirectly
by or for a qualified plan is not treated as outstanding.[13]
Furthermore, if the shareholder is a participant in the ESOP
or another qualified plan, qualified securities owned by or
for the person under the plan will be counted for purposes

of determining whether a person is a 25% or more share-holder.[14] In addition, stock owned by the shareholder's spouse, children, grandchildren, and parents will be attributed to the shareholder, as well as his or her proportionate share of stock owned by corporations controlled by him or her, partnerships in which he or she is a partner, and trusts of which he or she is either a beneficiary or a trustee.[15] If a prohibited allocation occurs, the securities will be deemed to have been distributed to the shareholder and the corporation will be subject to an additional tax of 50% of the amount involved.[16]

Reinvesting Sale Proceeds

To qualify for the 1042 tax deferral, the selling shareholder must purchase within a replacement period of 15 months, commencing 3 months before the date of sale and ending 12 months following the date of sale, securities issued by a domestic (i.e., U.S.-based) "operating corporation."[17] These securities are referred to as "qualified replacement property." Qualified replacement property does *not* include U.S. Treasury bills and notes, savings bonds, state and municipal bonds, other governmental obligations, certificates of deposit, or mutual funds.[18]

To constitute an "operating corporation," the corporation issuing securities that are deemed qualified replacement property must be a corporation:

- Organized under the laws of any state (or a U.S. subsidiary of a foreign corporation);

- More than 50% of the assets of which were used in the active conduct of a trade or business and which did not have passive investment income in excess of 25% of its gross income for the taxable year preceding the taxable year in which the purchase occurred;[19] and

- That is not the corporation that issued the qualified securities (that the qualified replacement property is replacing) or a member of the same controlled group of corporations.[20]

However, stocks and bonds of an insurance company subject to taxation or a bank that is subject by law to supervision and examination by a state or federal authority having supervision over banking institutions qualify as securities that the selling shareholder may purchase.[21]

Procedural Requirements for Tax Deferral

✔ **Statement of Election** To qualify for the 1042 tax deferral, the selling shareholder must affirmatively elect not to recognize the gain realized upon the sale of qualifying securities by filing a written "statement of election" with his or her tax return for the year in which the sale occurs, on or before the due date for filing such return.[22] The failure to file the statement of election, even if inadvertent, may preclude the taxpayer from obtaining the 1042 tax deferral.[23] Once made, the election is irrevocable.[24]

✔ **Statement of Purchase** In addition, following the purchase of qualified replacement property, the selling shareholder must sign a "statement of purchase," which to be valid must be notarized within the 15-month qualified election period referred to above and not later than the time the selling shareholder files his or her income tax return for the taxable year in which either (1) the sale of qualified securities occurred or (2) the purchase of the qualified replacement property occurred (whichever is applicable).[25] It should be noted that while the filing of a statement of election is a statutory requirement, and therefore compliance therewith will be strictly enforced, the execution of notarized statements of purchase is a regulatory requirement, and the taxpayer's inadvertent or unintentional noncompliance may be permitted under certain circumstances.[26]

✔ **Statement Consenting to Imposition of Excise Tax** In addition to the filings of the statement of election and notarized statements of purchase by the selling shareholder, the corporation (or the ESOP) must also submit, together with the selling shareholder's statement of election, a written statement consenting to (1) the imposition of a 10% additional tax if any qualified securities are sold or disposed of by the ESOP within three years following the date of sale (assessed on the amount realized on the disposition of the qualified securities)[27] and (2) the imposition of a 50% additional tax if the qualified securities are allocated to persons prohibited from receiving them.[28]

However, certain distributions, such as those made by reason of the death, disability, retirement after age 59½, or separation from service resulting from a one-year break in service, and distributions pursuant to stock-for-stock corporate reorganizations under Section 368(a)(1) of the Code, are exempt.[29] Distributions of qualified securities required to meet diversification requirements under Section 401(a)(28) of the Code also are exempt.[30]

When Deferred Tax Is Payable

Assuming the selling shareholder has affirmatively and validly elected the 1042 tax deferral and otherwise has complied with Section 1042's requirements, the selling shareholder will recognize and pay applicable tax on the gain realized in the transaction giving rise to the 1042 tax deferral when he or she sells or otherwise disposes of the qualified replacement property.[31] However, certain transfers and other dispositions will not trigger recapture of the realized gain, such as gifts[32] and transfers by reason of death.[33] Furthermore, recapture will not be triggered if the disposition occurs due to a tax-free reorganization of the issuer of the qualified replacement property[34] or a subsequent sale of the qualified replacement property by the selling shareholder in a transaction qualifying for tax deferral under Section 1042.[35]

Conclusion

Shareholders considering a sale of their closely held corporations have a number of options available to them. They can sell their stock or the assets of the corporation. They can sell for cash (in which case any gain realized will be taxable) or for stock of the acquiring corporation in a transaction structured as a tax-free reorganization. Each of these types of transactions has advantages, disadvantages, and tax consequences (a discussion of which is beyond the scope of this chapter).

However, when shareholders contemplate the sale of their stock in a closely held corporation, serious consideration should be given to a third alternative: a sale to an ESOP in a transaction structured under Section 1042 of the Code. The selling shareholders can receive cash equal to the fair market value of their stock and decide whether and to what extent they will take advantage of the unique opportunity to defer recognition of all (or any portion) of the gain realized in connection with the sale, by reinvesting all (or any portion) of the gain in qualified replacement property and recognizing taxable gain only on the portion not reinvested.

Of the many options available, selling to an ESOP and electing the 1042 tax deferral provides selling shareholders with the greatest flexibility in designing their personal financial and estate plans and an ownership succession plan necessary for the perpetuation, continued growth, and success of their corporations.

NOTES

1. Code § 1042. The election must be made by the taxpayer. Thus, if a partnership elects the 1042 tax deferral, the *partnership* must make the election and the *partnership* must purchase the qualified replacement property. See Technical Advisory Memorandum 9508001 (October 13, 1994); PLR 9846005 (November 13, 1998); PLR 200243001 (October 25, 2002).

2. See Code §§ 1042(c), 409(1). While the phrase "not readily tradable on an established securities market" is not defined in Code § 1042 (or Code § 409(l) [defining "employer securities"]), it is clear that if the corporation's stock were traded on a national or regional securities exchange or quoted by NASDAQ, such stock would not qualify as "qualified securities" and the 1042 tax deferral would be unavailable. Compare Treas. Reg. § 15A.453-1(e)(4) (defining the quoted phrase in the context of installment sales) with Treas. Reg. § 54.4975-7(b)(1)(4) (defining "publicly traded"). While in the great majority of cases a determination that a corporation's stock is not "readily tradable" will be relatively simple, in each case the nature of the security proposed to be

sold and the level of market activity in the stock should be examined. See, e.g., Private Letter Ruling (PLR) 8910067 (March 10, 1989) (Internal Revenue Service [IRS] permitted stock in which a local broker made a market to be "qualified securities" for purposes of the 1042 tax deferral); PLR 9219038 (February 12, 1992) (U.S. subsidiary's unlisted and untraded stock can be employer security despite foreign parent's shares being listed and traded on a foreign exchange).

3. See Code § 1042(c)(1)(B). But see PLR 9215026 (January 9, 1992) ("employer securities" may include (1) shares awarded to employees, the value of which were included in employee's income, and (2) § 1036 shares [i.e., shares of common stock exchanged for new shares of common stock in same corporation; under certain circumstances, the new shares (§ 1036 shares) may qualify for nonrecognition of gain] tendered to pay exercise price of option shares).

4. Code § 1042(b)(4).

5. See Code § 1223; Douglas Jaques, "'Tacking' On to the Section 1042 Seller's Holding Period," elsewhere in this book.

6. See Code § 1036.

7. See Code § 1036.

8. See Code § 368(a)(1); PLR200003014 (October 29, 1999) (holding period while S corporation election in effect tacked when ESOP formed after conversion to C corporation); PLR 9212013 (December 19, 1991) (tacking permitted for qualified securities received in certain merger and recapitalization transactions although the recapitalization exchange offer was conditioned on the sale of exchanged shares to the ESOP).

9. Code § 1042(b)(2); Treas. Reg. § 1.1042-IT Q&A-2(4)(b).

10. Code § 409(n)(1). See Brian Snarr, "The Prohibited Allocation Rule Under Section 1042," elsewhere in this book.

11. Code § 409(n)(1)(3).

12. Code § 409(n)(1)(B).

13. See Treas. Reg. § 1.1042-1T Q&A (2)(a)(3).

14. See Code § 409(n)(1)(B); IRS Announcement 95-33(III)(c)(b)(4). Compensation paid to shareholder-employees who are ineligible to share in an allocation in a taxable year may not be included in the calculation of total compensation paid or accrued during that taxable year when determining the amount of the corporation's tax deduction for plan contributions. See PLR 9442105 (July 18, 1994).

15. See Code § 318(a). This may not preclude a more-than-25% shareholder from receiving stock under an incentive stock option plan,

a non-qualified stock option plan, or a restricted stock plan that is not a qualified plan under Code § 401(a). See PLR 9442015 (July 18, 1994).

16. See Code § 4979A.

17. Code § 1042(c)(4).

18. See Code § 1042(c)(4)(D); PLR 9031044 (May 9, 1990) (regarding certificates of deposit).

19. Code §§ 1042(c)(4)(A)(i), 1042(c)(4)(B)(i). See PLR 200337003 (June 6, 2003) (newly formed S corporation in the business of buying, owning, leasing, and managing commercial real estate is operating corporation); See also PLR 9432009 (May 10, 1994) (corporate general partner of a limited partnership formed to develop and operate a commercial vineyard and which provides management services to limited partnership satisfied passive investment income test requirement).

20. Code § 1042(c)(4)(A)(ii). But see PLR 9429017 (April 25, 1994) (although company issuing qualified replacement property failed the passive investment income test when viewed alone, company would satisfy test when aggregated with affiliated corporation that is member of same controlled group, and therefore stock issued by company constitutes qualified replacement property).

21. See Code § 1042(c)(4)(B)(ii).

22. See Code § 1042(a)(1); Treas. Reg. § 1.1042-1T Q&A-3. The statement of election must affirmatively state that 1042 treatment is elected and must identify (1) the date of sale; (2) the type and amount of qualified securities sold; (3) the selling shareholder's adjusted basis; (4) the amount realized from the sale; and (5) the identity of the ESOT purchasing the qualified securities.

23. See PLR 9430816 (June 24, 1994) (filing of a statement of election, being a statutory requirement, will be strictly enforced).

24. See Treas. Reg. § 1.1042-1T Q&A-3.

25. Treas. Reg. § 1.1042-1T Q&A-3(c), as amended by Prop. Treas. Reg. 121122-03, 68 FR 41087-41089, 2003-37 IRB 550 (July 10, 2003). The statement of purchase must describe the qualified replacement property, the date it was purchased, and its cost, and affirmatively declare that the securities purchased constitute qualified replacement property with respect to the sale of qualified securities. If qualified replacement property has been purchased before the filing of the statement of election and during the qualified election period, all notarized statements of purchase must be attached. Otherwise, notarized statements of purchase must be filed with the selling shareholder's income tax return filed for the year following the year for which the 1042 election was made. Id.

26. Compare *Clause, John W., Estate of et al. v. Commissioner,* 122 TC 5, 32 EBC 2650 (USTC February 9, 2004) (1042 election invalid for noncompliance with statutory requirements), with PLR 200423018 (June 4, 2004, PLR 200324013 and PLR 9429017 (April 25, 1994) (taxpayers were granted relief from failure to have statement of purchase executed and notarized within 30-day period; statement of purchase was executed before deadline for filing of statement of election). See also PLR 200339010 (September 26, 2003) (substantial compliance by notarizing statement of purchase within 30 days of last purchase of qualified replacement property).

27. Code §§ 1042(b)(3), 4978(a)-(b).

28. See Code § 4979A and the text accompanying notes 14 and 15 above.

29. Code § 4978(d)(1)-(2).

30. Code § 1042(d)(4).

31. Code § 1042(e).

32. See Code § 1042(e)(3)(C). The term "gift" is not defined for purposes of Code § 1042(e)(3) and, as a result, the IRS has determined that recapture will not apply to transfers of qualified replacement property (1) to a trust qualifying as a grantor trust (see, e.g., PLRs 9224038 [March 16, 1992] and 9226027 [March 26, 1992]); (2) from a trust to a beneficiary under the trust (see, e.g., PLR 9411003 [December 8, 1993]); and (3) to a charitable remainder trust (see, e.g., PLRs 9234023 [May 26, 1992], 9438012 [June 22, 1994], 9438021 [June 27, 1994]). While the use of charitable remainder trusts following transactions to which Code § 1042 applies is beyond the scope of this chapter, for more information the reader may review Robert Schatz, "Give and Ye Shall Receive: ESOPs, Charitable Remainder Trusts and Life Insurance Trusts," *The ESOP Report* (February 1994).

33. Code § 1042(e)(3)(B). Note that upon the selling shareholder's death, the value of any qualified replacement property is included as part of the gross estate and, if bequeathed to the selling shareholder's spouse, should not be subject to estate tax by reason of the marital deduction. See Code §§ 2056, 2032(b), 1016(c).

34. See Code §§ 1042(e)(3)(A), 368(a).

35. Code § 1042(e)(3)(D).

10

SELLER-FINANCED ESOPs AND LEVERAGED QRP TRANSACTIONS

BRUCE F. BICKLEY
JAMES G. STEIKER

The key motivation for many ESOP transactions in closely held companies is the ability of the selling shareholder to defer capital gains tax on sale of shares to an ESOP under Section 1042 of the Internal Revenue Code (the "Code"). Section 1042 requires as a condition of capital gains tax deferral that upon completion of the sale, the ESOP own at least 30% of the outstanding shares of each class of company stock or stock representing 30% of the value of all company stock. At this time, the Section 1042 tax deferral is available only to selling owners in C corporations, not S corporations.

Section 404 of the Code imposes significant limitations, as a percentage of participant compensation, on how much may be contributed to an ESOP in a single year. Most ESOP transactions in closely held companies are therefore leveraged, as very few companies have a significant enough payroll base that 30% of the company's stock can be contributed to participants in a single year in compliance with applicable Section 404 limits on tax-deductible contributions to an ESOP. In a leveraged transaction, the ESOP uses borrowed money to acquire a significant block of company stock and promises to repay the loan from future company contributions.

Often, the ESOP borrows from an outside lender, such as a bank, to obtain the funds to buy company stock. However, sellers may prefer to finance the ESOP transaction themselves, either because they want to avoid bank financing (due to cost or other considerations) or because it is simply difficult or impossible to obtain bank financing. Under this approach, the selling shareholders receive a note from the ESOP as payment for some or all of the sale price. This chapter will discuss seller financing, its advantages and disadvantages, and the use of "leveraged QRP."

Rationale of Seller Financing

One condition of Section 1042 capital gains deferral is that the selling shareholder purchase "qualified replacement property" (QRP) with a value equal to the amount received in the qualifying ESOP transaction. (The shareholder can choose to purchase QRP equal to only part of the amount received, in which case the shareholder will pay taxes on the remainder of the proceeds.) QRP can include the stock and bonds of most, but not all, domestic operating corporations. It does not include mutual funds, real estate investment trusts (REITs), or government bonds. The selling shareholder defers capital gains tax until sale or other taxable disposition of the QRP. Banks generally consider the QRP to be purchased by a selling shareholder as excellent collateral for an ESOP loan.

Selling shareholders generally view a pledge of QRP or other seller guarantees of bank ESOP financing as creating a level of personal risk similar to providing the financing for the transaction themselves. Moreover, the company or the ESOP usually do not provide additional compensation to the selling shareholder in exchange for the pledge of QRP or the guarantee. The question is often framed as, "Why shouldn't I (the selling shareholder) collect the interest rather than the bank?"

Structure of Seller Financing

Most ESOP transactions use a "mirror loan" format. The lender makes a loan to the company and the company makes a loan to the ESOP to finance purchase of company stock from a shareholder. This structure can be followed where the lender is the selling shareholder, but is not always desirable.

In a mirror loan structure, the company makes a loan to the ESOP, and the ESOP uses the proceeds of the loan to purchase shares from a shareholder. The shareholder makes a loan to a company, and the company issues a note to the shareholder. The advantage of this structure is that the holder of the note has direct recourse to company assets, some technical legal issues concerning "fraudulent conveyance" are avoided, and there may be advantageous timing differences between the company's payment of contributions or tax-deductible dividends to the ESOP to repay the loan and the company's payment of the obligations under the note. For example, a company with extra cash would pay off the external loan faster, using a slower schedule to pay off the seller, either to avoid Section 404 deduction limit problems or to stretch out allocations to include more future employees. The disadvantage of this structure is that a shareholder who does not elect capital gains deferral under Section 1042 may not elect installment sale tax treatment as an alternative based on the deferred note payments. In other words, the seller will be taxed on the proceeds.

The deferred payments to the shareholder may be structured as a direct obligation of the ESOP. Usually, the company will provide an additional guarantee of the note from the ESOP. In this scenario, a shareholder who does not elect Section 1042 capital gains deferral may instead elect installment sale treatment with respect to the proceeds of the note. The balance sheet treatment of the ESOP obligation on the financial statements of the company is unaffected by whether the company provides a guarantee of the ESOP's obligation.

A selling shareholder providing seller financing and electing Section 1042 may accomplish direct recourse against the ESOP sponsor if desired. The selling shareholder may exchange a direct note from the ESOP for a similar note from the ESOP sponsor. Alternatively, the selling shareholder may borrow funds for a single day and loan the proceeds to the

ESOP sponsor at closing in exchange for a note. The ESOP sponsor then loans the funds to the ESOP and the ESOP nominally pays cash for the selling shareholder's stock at closing. The selling shareholder then uses the proceeds of the sale of stock to the ESOP to repay the "one-day" loan. The net result is that the selling shareholder has a note from the ESOP sponsor rather than the ESOP itself. The inability to obtain installment sales treatment is irrelevant if the selling shareholder is deferring capital gains tax under Section 1042.

Section 1042 Considerations

Section 1042 requires, as a condition of capital gains deferral, that the selling shareholder purchase QRP during the 15-month period commencing 3 months before and ending 12 months after the date of a qualifying sale to an ESOP. This period is not extended by the ESOP's payment of the purchase price for the shares in the form of a note.

This creates a dilemma for a shareholder who is otherwise willing to sell shares to an ESOP in exchange for a note. Payment of the sale proceeds to the shareholder may occur over several years. Purchase of the QRP must, however, take place within one year of the date of sale. For a shareholder who receives a note as payment in an ESOP transaction to elect capital gains deferral under Section 1042, he or she must use other available funds to purchase QRP during the applicable period. (The IRS ruled in Private Letter Ruling 9102017 that the money used to buy QRP need not be the actual sale proceeds.) Relatively few shareholders have sufficient liquid assets to accomplish this funding.

Use of Leveraged Qualified Replacement Securities

Section 1042 concerns based on a need for short-term funds to purchase QRP may be addressed by purchase of QRP that may be used as collateral for a margin loan at a relatively high loan-to-value. The major brokerage houses will typically offer margin loans on securities without other collateral at specified ratios and at or near the "broker call" rate. Advance ratios against stocks are 50%, while advance ratios against debt instruments (e.g. bonds) range from 70% to 75% depending on whether the coupon is fixed or floating. (Banks are not subject to the same margin restrictions that brokerage houses are, so with a bank the advance ratio against a stock could be over 50%.) The broker call rate reflects short-term interest rates and varies at around 0.5 to 2.0 percentage points below the prime rate. If the value of the underlying margined security drops, the brokerage house may make a "margin call" requiring sufficient repayment of the loan such that the advance ratios described above are not exceeded.

The desired attributes of the QRP are therefore (1) a debt instrument (to maximize the potential amount of the margin loan), (2) high safety and credit quality (to reduce risk and price fluctuations based upon the creditworthiness of the issuer), (3) a long maturity and call protection (so that the capital gain deferred on sale of shares to the ESOP will not be recognized upon maturity or call of the debt instrument), and (4) a floating interest rate (to avoid price fluctuations and potential margin calls based upon changes in underlying interest rate conditions).

Several brokerage houses offer a form of QRP with these attributes called a "Floating Rate Note" (FRN). These securities, generally issued by large corporations, have high credit ratings, normally AAA or AA, and a floating interest rate, therefore insuring relative price stability and security. The term of the notes usually range from 30 to 60 years. It is relatively easy to purchase this security with a down payment of as little as 10% of the underlying value of the FRN, with financing from a lending institution or a broker.

✔ **Example of Seller-Financed ESOP with Leveraged QRP** The following example illustrates the use of leveraged QRP in a seller-financed Section 1042 ESOP transaction:

1. Seller sells $10 million stock to the ESOP in exchange for $1 million cash and a note for the $9 million balance (the proportion of cash and note may vary).

2. Within 12 months of sale date, Seller deposits $1 million cash proceeds with an outside bank or brokerage house ("Lender").

3. Simultaneously, Seller purchases $10 million as QRP under Section 1042.

4. Lender loans Seller $9 million on (30-day) LIBOR-based rate secured by pledge of FRN.

5. Seller receives ongoing payments from ESOP as principal and interest on Seller note. Seller may use payments to reduce Lender loan or may otherwise invest or spend proceeds.

The net cash flow of interest from these transactions is illustrated below:

Sample applicable rates (as of September 2004):

Seller note @ prime + 2	6.25%
FRN yield @30-day LIBOR – 25 basis points	1.75%
Bank loan secured by FRN @ *30-day* LIBOR + 50 basis points	2.50%

First-year interest cash flow:

Seller note interest income ($9 million @ 4.25%)	$562,500
FRN income ($10 million @ 1.75%)	175,000
Less: Interest expense to Lender ($9 million @ 2.50%)	225,000
Net interest income	$512,500

(First-year effective yield = 5.69%)

Pros and Cons of Seller Financing

Seller financing is especially appropriate for consideration in a Section 1042 transaction where the seller will likely pledge all of the QRP to be acquired with the proceeds of the transaction as collateral to the lender. Seller financing may provide a greater financial return relative to risk as the seller may capture a premium representing the gap between the rate charged by a lender on a loan collateralized by QRP and the rate a seller may command as a "reasonable rate" on the seller note. Seller financing, when appropriately subordinated, may help companies subject to bonding or other balance-sheet related credit tests, where the outside bonding agency or creditor might view bank financing as excessive leverage. Seller financing may also provide greater flexibility to structure a leveraged transaction around seasonal or fluctuating cash flow. Seller-financed transactions are also less expensive to accomplish and require less documentation and due diligence.

Seller financing using leveraged QRP may subject the seller to an underlying lack of diversification if one were to invest 100% in a single security. Sellers can use the proceeds from the note to purchase a diversified portfolio of investments, but they will do so over time. In essence, the sellers would be dollar-cost averaging into the market, buying fewer shares when stock prices are high and more shares when prices are low. During a period of rising stock prices, the rate of return on the notes, even with the positive interest float from the ESOP note to the seller, will be below the typical rate of return on equities; thus, the seller would lose out on the opportunities a Section 1042 transaction provides to get this higher rate sooner by investing immediately. For example, if a seller elects Section 1042 treatment and invests in equities with a 10% annual return, that seller will be better off than one who invests in a FRN with an effective rate of 5.69% (adding in the extra interest from the note to the seller).

A selling shareholder may also find it difficult to balance his or her lender concerns against his or her management or ownership concerns if the company experiences difficulty in making timely repayment of the seller note. Additionally, bank financing imposes discipline and due diligence on a company to ensure that the projected ESOP debt is appropriate and that there are no other concerns that militate against the proposed ESOP transaction.

However, the leveraged QRP approach allows a seller who cannot obtain, or does not want to obtain, bank financing to elect Section 1042 treatment on the entire amount of the sale proceeds.

Conclusion

Seller financing may be a desirable alternative to conventional bank financing; it also may provide a level of subordinated debt to achieve a desired debt package in certain leveraged ESOP transactions. If the seller desires to elect Section 1042 treatment but needs short-term funds to purchase QRP within the required 15-month period, the leveraged QRP approach described here can be used to provide those funds within the context of seller financing.

11

ARE ESOP FLOATING RATE NOTES RIGHT FOR YOU?

COREY ROSEN

Sellers to ESOPs that own at least 30% of a C corporation's stock can, under Section 1042 of the Internal Revenue Code, "roll over" and reinvest their gains in qualified replacement investments and defer capital gains taxes until the replacement investments are sold. For many people, that means buying a long-term portfolio of investments. Other sellers, however, want to pursue a more active investment strategy, but if they do that with their portfolio, each time they sell a security, they have to pay tax on the share of the gain that represents from both the reinvestment and the original sale to the ESOP. In 1987, a solution to this problem was created when special very long-term, non-callable bonds (called "ESOP notes") were made available as qualified replacement investments. Because they were not likely to expire or be called during the seller's lifetime, no capital gains tax would be paid. Because they were in highly rated companies, owners of the bonds could borrow as much as 90% of their face value to reinvest in actively managed portfolios. In recent years, the bonds have also been marketed as a solution for owners who take a note from the ESOP when they sell rather than using an outside lender. The seller can borrow to buy the bond, then repay the loan with the payments from the note, thus qualifying the installment sale for tax deferral.

This chapter looks at some of the pros and cons of the ESOP note strategy.

How ESOP Notes Work

ESOP notes are non-callable 30- to 60-year bonds paying a floating rate of interest (ESOP notes are also called Floating-Fate Notes, or FRNs). Their yield is based on the 30- or 90-day London Interbank Offered Rate (LIBOR). ESOP notes currently are about 10-45 basis points (one basis point is .01 percent) below LIBOR, depending on their credit quality, for a current yield of about 0.65% to 1%. Ten-year U.S. Treasury bonds currently yield about 4.3%, by comparison. Interest rates currently charged to borrow against these notes are currently about 0.4% to 1.0% over LIBOR, depending on the size of the bond and other factors.

The notes can be bought in denominations as small as $1,000, but they would be very hard for the investor to sell in these small amounts. Experts advise buying the notes in at least $100,000 units. Transaction costs for the note itself are low or none, as the issuer incorporates the underwriting costs into the interest rate. There may be fees associated with a bank loan to buy these notes, however, if the notes are being used as part of a seller-financed transaction. Most borrowers can borrow 80% to 90% against these notes, but 100% is possible if other assets are used as collateral. To protect against an issuer going bankrupt, buyers should buy notes from several companies. A put option should be attached to the note (not all have this); it is possible at some point that a lack of ESOP sellers could make it difficult to sell the notes on the open market.

Investment Considerations

Several factors must be considered in making a decision to buy ESOP notes:

- Expected returns on passively managed portfolios vs. actively managed ones;
- The float on the difference between interest paid on the notes and borrowing costs;
- Foregone investment opportunities on whatever percentage (10% in most cases) of the note is not borrowed;

- Commissions and/or advisory fees on actively managed vs. passive portfolios;
- Current income needs;
- Transaction size; and
- Risks.

The ESOP note strategy assumes an actively managed portfolio can make a return on investment that is higher enough than a passive portfolio to compensate for the fact that it costs more to borrow against the note than the note pays in interest (this difference may be as much as 2% in the current market and could be more when interest rates are higher). If the buyer maintains 10% of the note as collateral, then the active portfolio must also overcome the very low rate of return on that 10%. An active portfolio also means more commission and fees than most passive portfolios because more securities are bought and sold. The net result of this is that the active portfolio must return a rate about 15% to 30% higher than the active portfolio (if the rate of return on a passive portfolio is 8%, the active portfolio must yield about 9% to 10.5%), depending on whose assumptions are used. Balanced against this is the likelihood of paying taxes on at least part of a passive portfolio's investments. Current capital gains rates are only 15% federal plus whatever the state tax (if any) is, but these rates fluctuate.

In general, the experts agree that the ESOP note approach works best for younger sellers who prefer to stay involved in the management of their assets. Smaller transactions (generally less than $1 million, but experts disagree on this) are not as practical because it is more difficult to put together a diversified portfolio of notes. People who need current income may also benefit given the greater flexibility of the active strategy.

CHAPTER **12**

"TACKING" ON TO THE SECTION 1042 SELLER'S HOLDING PERIOD

DOUGLAS JAQUES

Section 1042(b)(4) of the Internal Revenue Code (the "Code") requires that a selling shareholder have a holding period for the stock being sold to the ESOP of at least three years for the tax deferral contemplated under Section 1042 to be available. As originally enacted by the Deficit Reduction Act of 1984 (P.L. 98-369), Code Section 1042(a) required only that the stock have been held by the selling shareholder for one year, the minimum holding period for long-term capital gain tax treatment to be available. In the Omnibus Budget Reconciliation Act of 1989, perhaps in response to publicity about certain deferred sales to ESOPs following as soon as possible after the shareholders purchased the corporation, Congress added Section 1042(b)(4) of the Code.

In establishing the ESOP rules, Congress permitted the holding period of assets contributed to a corporation under Section 351 of the Code to be included as part of the original Code Section 1042 one-year holding period. The *General Explanation of the Deficit Reduction Act of 1984*, produced by the Joint Committee on Taxation, specifically states at page 875 that "qualified securities are defined as employer securities that . . . have been held by the seller for more than one year (which, pursuant to Treasury Regulations, includes periods otherwise permitted to be 'tacked' to the holding period under other Code provisions)." Similarly, the legislative history of Section 1042(b)(4) specifically states that "the rules relating to holding periods of property (Section 1223) apply in determining whether the three-year holding period requirement is satisfied." Based on the foregoing, Section 1223 should be applicable for determining the holding period under Section 1042(b)(4).

Assuming that a corporate contribution transaction qualifies for nonrecognition treatment under Section 351, a transferor's holding period in stock received will generally include the holding period of the assets contributed. Specifically, Section 1223(1) provides: "there shall be included the period for which [the taxpayer] held the property exchanged if . . . the property has . . . the same basis in whole or in part in his hands as the property exchanged."

Under Sections 351(b) and 358, the basis of stock received by a transferor in a good Section 351 transaction is the basis of the property contributed, increased by the amount of gain recognized by such transferor. Because the basis of such stock is determined "in whole or in part" with reference to the basis of the property exchanged for it, "tacking" of the exchanged property's holding period is permitted in determining the stock's holding period.

✔ **Example One**   A sole proprietor contributes a piece of machinery to a new corporation in exchange for all of its stock. The machinery had been owned by the sole proprietor for two years. The stock received in the new corporation will have a holding period of two years in the transferor's hands (as did the machinery). Accordingly, the stockholder of the new corporation will be able to satisfy the Section 1042(b)(4) three-year holding period requirement one year after the incorporation of his or her company.

The foregoing result under Section 1223(1), however, obtains only if the property transferred to the corporation is a "capital asset" (as defined in Section 1221) or Section 1231 property in the hands of the transferor. Section 1221 provides that a "capital asset" does not include stock in trade properly included in inventory, and accounts and notes receivable. Thus, no tacking is available for that portion of the stock received in a Section 351 transaction that is attributable to inventory or accounts receivable.

Even if an incorporation transaction is structured, as a matter of form, to specifically allocate non-stock consideration to non-capital assets, the IRS takes the position that non-stock consideration must be allocated among *all* property transferred for purposes of determining the holding period of the stock and other consideration received by the transferor.[1] Accordingly, unless accounts receivable and inventory and other property not constituting capital assets under Section 1221 are retained by the transferor and not contributed, the portion of the stock received in a Section 351 transaction attributable to such assets would have to be held for the full three-year period contemplated by Section 1042(b)(4). The foregoing rules and principles apply without regard to whether the transferor contributes real property, tangible personal property, or intangible property (such as stocks, securities, or the goodwill of an ongoing business), as long as such assets are capital assets.

✔ **Example Two**   The facts are the same as in Example One, except that the sole proprietor also wishes to transfer inventory to his or her new corporation. If inventory is transferred for stock, such stock will have a holding period beginning on the date of acquisition by the sole proprietor. If the sole proprietor were to structure the incorporation as a sale of the inventory for a note, and the contribution of the machinery as an exchange for stock, the IRS would nonetheless allocate the non-stock consideration among all property transferred. Accordingly, if inventory is transferred to the new corporation, a portion of the stock received will have a new holding period and will not be able to obtain the benefits of an ESOP transaction until three years after such receipt.

The facts described above are relatively simple in that the transferor is assumed to retain ownership of the stock received. It is not unusual, however, for a partnership to be the owner of the assets to be contributed to the new corporation and to wish to distribute the stock received to its partners. If a partnership transferor distributes to its partners stock that it receives in a Section 351 transaction, additional analysis is required to determine the holding period of such stock in the hands of the partners.

Whether such partnership distribution is in complete liquidation of such partnership or an operating distribution, Section 735(b) of the Code provides that in determining the holding period of the property distributed, "there shall be included the holding period of the partnership as determined under Section 1223."

If a partnership distribution follows a Section 351 transaction with the holding period consequences discussed above, the partnership's holding period will include the holding period of property transferred to the transferee corporation under Section 1223(1). The holding period of the distributee partner in the stock is thus determined with reference to the partnership's holding period in the property transferred to the corporation, *not* with reference to the partner's holding period in the partnership interest.

✔ **Example Three**   A partnership contributes a piece of machinery to a new corporation in exchange for all of its stock. The machinery had been owned by the partnership for two years. A 25% interest in the partnership had recently been acquired by a new partner. If such partnership were to distribute a portion of the stock received to the new partner, such partner would be able to satisfy the ESOP three-year holding period requirement one year after incorporation of the corporation notwithstanding the time that he or she had been a partner in the partnership.

The foregoing result may create significant opportunities for partners who are recent acquirors of an interest in a partnership that has held its assets for a significant period of time to bootstrap themselves into satisfying the Section 1042 holding period requirement.

Conclusion

The benefits of Code Section 1042 may be available even when shareholders have not held their stock for the minimum three-year period required by Section 1042(b)(4), due to the ability to include the period in which certain assets were held before their contributions to the corporation. These tacking rules even permit advance planning through an incorporation and a Section 351 contribution of assets, followed by a Section 1042 ESOP transaction. As a final note, care must be taken to comply with the "control immediately after" requirement of Code Section 351, a subject that is beyond the scope of this chapter.

NOTE

1. See Rev. Rul. 85-164, 1985-2 C.B. 117, amplifying Rev. Rul. 62-140, 1962-2 C.B. 181 and Rev. Rul. 68-55, 1968-1 C.B. 140 (the aggregate basis of different assets transferred in a § 351 transaction must be allocated among the consideration received in proportion to the relative fair market value of such consideration; the stock received has a split holding period).

13

QUALIFYING SELLERS FOR SECTION 1042 ROLLOVER TREATMENT WHEN THEY SELL TO ANOTHER COMPANY'S ESOP

COREY ROSEN

Leveraged ESOPs provide acquiring companies with a substantial tax benefit in that they can borrow money to make an acquisition and repay the loan in pretax dollars. But can the sellers of closely held companies qualify for Section 1042 treatment as well when selling to an ESOP? Until recently, the answer was "yes," but the route to get there was quite complicated. A January 28, 1998, IRS ruling, however, appeared to create a very straightforward way to accomplish this objective. While ESOP experts believe that the ruling does clear the way for straightforward ESOP transactions in these circumstances, however, the ruling was not specifically about ESOPs and has not been tested with reference to them. Moreover, IRS activities subsequent to the ruling have suggested that it may decide not to allow this approach, so advisors should follow this area closely. This chapter will start with an explanation of how sellers acquired 1042 treatment prior to the January 1998 ruling and end with a description of how the ruling would greatly simplify the process.

Before proceeding, however, keep in mind that for this approach to work, the seller must still meet the standard qualifications that would apply in any 1042 transaction, namely that the ESOP end up owning at least 30% of the company's shares (in this case, the consolidated company); the ESOP must be in a closely held C corporation; and the owner must have owned the shares for at least three years, or an equivalent sole proprietorship or partnership interest that is or has been converted to shares before the sale.

The Situation Before January 1998

There were two key stumbling blocks before the January 1998 ruling. One related to the three-year holding period required of the seller in order to qualify for Section 1042 treatment; the other related to the requirement that the ESOP hold at least 30% of the company's share after the transaction. Tax rules that applied to mergers and acquisitions in general made it very difficult to meet these requirements.

✔ **The Stock Must Have Been Held for Three Years** The owner of the target company must have held the securities he or she is selling to the ESOP (or other securities that qualify through "tacking" provisions that treat them as equivalent, such as ownership of preferred shares converted to common in the same company) for at least three years before the transaction. So if the acquiring company ("Company A") has its ESOP buy stock of the owner of the target company ("Company B"), that would not meet the three-year test. Moreover, the securities sold to the ESOP must be "employer securities" of the employer that sponsors the ESOP, not securities of another employer unrelated to the plan sponsor at the time of the sale.

✔ **Having the Seller Sell to the ESOP of the Target Company (Company "B"), Then Sell the Company to an Acquiring Company (Company "A"), Would Not Work** The problem here is that the Employee Retirement Income Security Act of 1974 (ERISA) requires that when there is a Section 1042 sale, the ESOP's ownership cannot drop below 30% of the company for three years. Repurchases from departing employees or a tax-free exchange of company stock for stock in another company do not count. So the acquisition of Company "B" by Company "A" within three years of the owner of "B" selling to "B's" ESOP would create a violation unless it could be accomplished by a tax-free exchange. If the rule is violated, the target company ("B") would have to pay a 10% excise tax on the transaction, a cost the acquiring company would end up paying. The seller is unlikely to want to wait three years so the sale would qualify, and even then the seller could not require the ESOP of the acquiring company to buy the shares at all, much less at an agreed-on price.

Methods That Work

✔ **Straightforward Acquisition**   Until January 28, 1998, it appeared the only way to provide the target's seller with 1042 treatment was a reverse merger or having both companies set up ESOPs and then having them merged. These relatively complex approaches are described below. A much simpler approach now appears possible, however.

In this approach, the acquirer merges with the target, with the owner of the target taking shares in the acquirer as consideration for the value of his or her ownership. These shares can then be sold to the acquirer's ESOP, and the seller can take Section 1042 treatment. The key element of this approach is that the ESOP be considered an "unrelated third party." In some other aspects of tax taw, an ESOP is considered an unrelated third party. For instance, if Section 1042 is not elected in an ESOP sale, the seller still qualifies for capital gains treatment because the ESOP is considered an unrelated third party (which is required for such treatment). This solves the problems outlined above. The owner meets the three-year test because the shares in the acquirer are considered the equivalent of the shares held in the owner's business. The three-year post-transaction holding period rule is met as long as the ESOP in the acquirer does not dispose of shares in sufficient quantity to bring it below 30%. This is again because the shares in the seller's company, now exchanged for shares in the acquiring company, are considered equivalent.

The January 1998 IRS ruling, however, did not specifically say that sales to an ESOP in the scenario described here would qualify. While this appears to be likely and some transactions using this model have been completed, careful consultation with counsel is required.

✔ **Merging the Target into the Acquiring Company**   Unlike a sale to the target company's ESOP (which, as described above, would not work) in this case the acquiring company would merge the target into it first. This could be done through a tax-free reorganization under Section 368 of the Internal Revenue Code. That section requires, however, that there be a "continuity of business enterprise" and a "continuity of interest" by shareholders in the merged entity. A merger envisioned here would meet the first test, but the second requires that any shareholders in the companies being merged retain at least a 50% ownership interest for at least two years (there have been some rulings allowing a lower percentage, but this is a safer number). So the owner of the target could sell 50% of his or her stock to the ESOP and take the rollover, but not the other 50% until two years had passed. At that point, however, there would be no guarantee the ESOP would buy the shares, or buy them at a set price. Even giving the ESOP an option to buy the shares would probably make the merger taxable.

✔ **Using a Reverse Merger**   In this approach, the acquisition company is merged into the target company first. The new company would meet both the "continuity of business" test, assuming its business was still operated by the acquiring firm, and the "continuity of interest" test. Because the latter test would apply now only to the shareholders of the acquiring firm (their shares are being exchanged for the target's), as long as they do not sell 50% or more of the stock in two years, the test is met. Meanwhile, the new company could immediately reassume the name of the firm that wants to do the acquisition. The owner of the target can now sell to the ESOP and take advantage of Section 1042, assuming the requirement of having the ESOP own 30% of the total shares in the merged company is met.

This approach adds a layer of complexity to the transaction, and hence adds costs. It should not be significantly more costly than any other acquisition strategy, however, and could make it possible for the acquiring firm to pay a lower price if the seller gives back part of the tax benefits.

✔ **Setting Up ESOPs in Both the Target and Acquiring Companies** While the reverse merger is the approach most commonly recommended, some consultants report success with another approach that involves both the target and acquiring company setting up ESOPs. Typically, the acquirer will have had an ESOP in place well before the transaction. The target company's owner sells to the target ESOP in a transaction that may be financed by the acquirer and takes Section 1042 treatment. Immediately thereafter, the acquiring company's ESOP merges with the target's ESOP. Typically, the acquiring company's ESOP would now own a majority of the target's shares (because the ESOP in the target had at least a majority), so that the target company ESOP participants can now participate in the ESOP of the acquiring company because the target is a member of the acquirer's control group. In theory, this could work even if the target's ESOP owned less than 50% of target's shares and the ESOPs in the two companies were merged into a "multiple employer ESOP" (a rare and unwieldy, but legal, creation). No one we know of has used this latter approach, however. Subsequently (at least one or two years later), the two companies merge. The delay is necessary to meet the rules governing tax-free reorganizations, although there may be specific exemptions for unusual circumstances.

This approach has been used in at least one transaction that received a private letter ruling from the IRS, but most practitioners believe it will be less common than reverse mergers. Both approaches are complex and require the advice of people specifically experienced in these issues.

14

THE PROHIBITED ALLOCATION RULE UNDER SECTION 1042

BRIAN B. SNARR

In allowing the tax-deferred "rollover" under Section 1042 of the Internal Revenue Code of 1986, as amended (the "Code"),[1] Congress sought to encourage broad-based employee ownership by providing business owners with a powerful inducement to sell their stock to an ESOP.[2] To make sure this potent incentive promotes the intended goal of employee ownership rather than encouraging tax-enhanced stock transfers to the family members and business partners of the business owners, Congress also imposed the "prohibited allocation rule" now found in Code Section 409(n). As with many rules in the Code, the prohibited allocation rule is not a model of clarity. This chapter sets forth the rule in a format intended to allow the reader to answer the question, "Does the prohibited allocation rule apply in my situation?"

Briefly, Section 409(n)(1)(A) prohibits, for no less than 10 years after an ESOP purchases shares from a shareholder who makes a Section 1042 rollover, any allocation under the ESOP attributable to those shares, either for the benefit of the selling shareholder or for any individuals "related" to him or her. Section 409(n)(1)(B) also prohibits such allocations for the benefit of any participant who owns (or is considered to own under attribution rules) over 25% of any class of the employer corporation's stock.

When Does the Prohibited Allocation Rule Apply?

The prohibited allocation rule applies only when an ESOP has purchased employer securities from a shareholder who has satisfied the requirements for a Section 1042 rollover. Consequently, when there is only one selling shareholder, the shareholder and any related parties can fully participate in the ESOP if the shareholder does *not* make the Section 1042 rollover. However, if there are multiple selling shareholders, the situation can become more complicated if even one of them makes the Section 1042 rollover. The more-than-25% shareholder rule (discussed below) can prevent even a shareholder who does not make the election from receiving ESOP allocations attributable to the Section 1042 shares.

What happens if a selling shareholder attempts to make the Section 1042 rollover, but fails, for example, where the 30% ESOP ownership requirement of Section 1042 is not met or where the shareholder fails to make a timely 1042 election? The prohibited allocation rule is applicable by its terms only to assets "acquired by the plan . . . in a sale to which section 1042 applies."[3] If Section 1042 does not apply because of a failure to meet its requirements, the prohibited allocation rule will not apply either. If the Section 1042 rollover is partly effective and partly ineffective, the prohibited allocation rule will still apply, because Section 1042 would still be partly applicable.

To Whom Does the Prohibited Allocation Rule Apply? ("Restricted Persons")

This is often the most difficult question in applying the prohibited allocation rule, because the attribution rules widen the nonallocation net to include related parties and persons whose ownership may be constructive rather than actual. The individuals affected by the prohibited allocation rule are referred to in this chapter as "restricted persons."

✔ **The Selling Shareholder** A person who has made a Section 1042 rollover cannot receive an allocation attributable to the employer securities sold to the ESOP. This is an understandable limitation, given the purpose of Section 1042. The former shareholder has already received such a substantial tax benefit on the rollover that getting his or her shares back from the ESOP on a further tax-deferred basis was considered by Congress to be excessive.

In a 1990 private letter ruling involving multiple selling shareholders, all of whom made the Section 1042 rollover, the Internal Revenue Service (IRS) held that they were all prevented from receiving allocations attributable to 1042 employer securities, even where one shareholder's allocation of employer securities was demonstrably purchased from a different selling shareholder.[4]

However, a selling shareholder who has made a Section 1042 rollover should be permitted to receive unrestricted allocations under an ESOP sponsored by an unrelated employer, provided the prohibited allocation rule does not apply for a different reason (for example, because the shareholder is related to a selling shareholder in the other ESOP or is subject to the 25% shareholder limitation). Also, as discussed below under "Exceptions to the Prohibited Allocation Rule," the rule does not apply to shares as to which the Section 1042 election was *not* made.

✔ **Certain Relatives of the Selling Shareholder** Once a shareholder sells employer securities to an ESOP and makes a Section 1042 rollover, the prohibited allocation rule prevents allocations to individuals related to the selling shareholder within the meaning of Code Section 267(b).[5] Only individuals related to a selling shareholder who makes the Section 1042 rollover will be affected.[6] Individuals related to a selling shareholder who does not make the Section 1042 rollover will not be affected (unless the more-than-25% shareholder rule applies to them).

Following is a list of the individuals who are considered to be related to a selling shareholder, as listed in Section 267(b):

- *Brothers and sisters.* The selling shareholder's half brothers and sisters count as brothers and sisters.[7]

- *Spouse.* The selling shareholder's legal spouse, including a separated spouse if there is no annulment or final decree of divorce.

- *Ancestors.* Ancestors include the selling shareholder's parents, grandparents, and great grandparents.

- *Lineal descendants.* They include the selling shareholder's children, grandchildren, and great grandchildren. Legally adopted children are considered children for this purpose.[8]

- *Trust beneficiaries.* Such a relationship exists when a trust sells shares to an ESOP and makes the Section 1042 rollover,[9] and a trust beneficiary is employed by the ESOP sponsor.[10]

- *Estate beneficiaries.* Such a relationship exists when an estate sells shares to an ESOP and makes the Section 1042 rollover, and an estate beneficiary is employed by the ESOP sponsor.

- *Partners.* If a partnership sells employer securities to an ESOP and makes the Section 1042 rollover, any partners employed by the ESOP sponsor will be subject to the prohibited allocation rule.[11] Family members (brothers, sisters, spouse, ancestors, and lineal descendants) of such a partner who are employed by the ESOP sponsor would also be affected.[12]

The prohibited allocation rule applies only to individuals because entities cannot participate in an ESOP. Accordingly, many related-party relationships specified in Section 267(b) are not applicable in the context of the prohibited allocation rule because they apply to entities.

The following persons are not related for purposes of the prohibited allocation rule that applies to selling shareholders:

- *Aunts and uncles.*[13]

- *Nieces and nephews.*[14]

- *Stepchildren.*[15]

- *Stepparents.*[16]

- *In-laws.*[17] They include parents-in-law, sons- and daughters-in-law, and brothers- and sisters-in-law.

✔ **More-Than-25% Shareholders** Once a shareholder sells employer securities to an ESOP and makes the Section 1042 rollover, the prohibited allocation rule prevents allocations of such shares to any shareholder holding more than 25% of any class of stock of the issuing corporation and certain related corporations. The most significant effect of the more-than-25% shareholder rule is that shareholders who do not sell shares, or who sell shares but do not make the Section 1042 rollover, are still limited in their ability to participate in the ESOP.

A person will be considered a more-than-25% owner for this purpose if he or she owns, actually or constructively under the attribution rules of Code Section 318, more than (1) 25% of any class of stock of the corporation issuing the employer securities that were sold; (2) 25% of any class of stock of any corporation that is a member of the same controlled group as the corporation issuing the employer securities; (3) 25% of the value of any class of stock of the corporation that issued the employer securities; or (4) 25% of the value of any corporation that is a member of the same controlled group as the corporation issuing the employer securities.[18]

There are two times when a person's shareholdings (actual and constructive) must be considered to determine his or her status as a 25% shareholder: first, at the time of the sale to the ESOP (and in the one-year period before the sale), and second, at the time shares are actually allocated to ESOP participants.[19]

In determining whether a person is subject to the prohibited allocation rule because of the more-than-25% shareholder rule, the person's own shareholdings in the employer corporation are, of course, taken into account. In addition, a person must add to his or her actual shareholdings (if any) the shares owned by the following persons specified in Section 318:

- *A spouse.* An ESOP participant must include in his or her shareholdings all shares owned by the participant's legal spouse, including a separated spouse where there is no annulment or final decree of divorce.

- *Children.* An ESOP participant's adopted children as well as biological children must be included.[20]

- *Grandchildren.*

- *Parents.*

- *Partnerships.* A member of a partnership is considered to own his or her proportionate share of any stock in the employer corporation owned by the partnership.[21] For example, if A is a 40% partner in partnership ABC that owns 100 shares of Corporation E, A will be considered to own 40 shares of Corporation E. However, stock owned by one partner, although it is considered owned by the partnership, is not considered therefore to be owned by the other partners.[22]

- *S corporations.* The shareholder of an S corporation is considered to own his or her proportionate share of any stock in the employer corporation owned by the S corporation.[23] S corporations thus follow the partnership rule rather than the usual corporate attribution rule.

- *Estates.* Stock of an employer corporation owned by an estate is considered to be owned proportionately by its beneficiaries.[24] This includes persons entitled to receive property under a will or through intestate succession.[25] Thus, estate beneficiaries must include their estate legacies in calculating whether they are more-than-25% shareholders.[26]

- *Trusts.* A trust beneficiary is considered to own stock owned by a trust in proportion to his or her actuarial interest in the trust.[27] This actuarial calculation is performed under a method prescribed in regulations.[28]

- *Grantor trusts.* A grantor is considered to own any stock owned by the trust that he or she would be considered to own under the grantor trust rules.[29] The same rule applies to any other person considered to be the owner of the trust assets under the grantor trust rules.

- *Employee plans.* Any stock owned by the trust established under a qualified plan (profit-sharing, pension, stock bonus plan, or ESOP) is considered to be owned in proportion to the participants' actuarial interests, under the usual trust attribution rules.[30] The Senate Report to the 1986 Tax Reform Act states that in an ESOP, only allocated shares are taken into account.[31]

- *Corporations.* If one corporation owns shares of an employer corporation, then shareholders of the owner corporation are considered to own stock in the employer corporation only if the owner corporation holds 50% or more (in value) of the employer corporation.[32] When the 50% ownership threshold is met, the shareholders of the owner corporation are considered to own the stock in the employer corporation in the same proportion (by value) that they own shares of the owner corporation.[33]

- *Options.* A person who has an option to acquire stock is considered to have exercised the option and to own the stock that is subject to the option.[34] This includes stock that can be acquired under options, warrants, or conversion privileges, so long as there is no condition or contingency on exercise that has not been met.[35]

✔ **Reattribution and Its Limits**   In calculating a person's stock ownership for the more-than-25% shareholder rule, the attribution rules of Section 318 require counting the ownership of certain other parties. In calculating the ownership of these other parties, it is necessary to consider not only the shares they actually own, but also certain shares that are attributed to them. For example, if a shareholder's daughter owns 500 shares of Employer Corp. in her own name and is a one-third partner in a partnership that owns an additional 1,500 shares, the shareholder will have 1,000 shares (500 + [1,500 ÷ 3]) attributed to him or her from the daughter. This is referred to as "reattribution," which significantly complicates the job of figuring out who owns what. However, the reattribution rules have several limits that prevent attribution from proceeding *ad infinitum.*

First, many of the attribution rules that might otherwise apply under Section 318, for example, by causing a partnership to be considered the owner of stock owned by one of its partners, are simply not relevant when the only issue is whether an individual is considered the owner of more than 25% of a corporation's stock.

Next, in determining a person's constructive ownership under Section 318, another person's stock can be counted only once for attribution purposes, although it will be counted in the manner that imputes the largest total stock ownership.[36] For example, if Wife owns 1,000 shares of Employer Corp. stock and Husband and Son own no shares, Husband and Son will each be considered to own 1,000 shares attributed from Wife. Although Husband's 1,000 attributed shares would usually be further attributed to both Wife and Son, for a total of 3,000 for her and 2,000 for him, they cannot be counted more than once for any one person because all the attribution is based on the same 1,000 shares.

Finally, due to limitations in the attribution and constructive ownership rules of Section 318, there are certain related persons whose stock holdings are *not* considered in determining whether an ESOP participant is a more-than-25% shareholder:

- *Grandchildren.*[37] Although grandchildren are not considered to own stock owned by their grandparents, as noted above, grandparents *are* considered to own any stock owned by their grandchildren.
- *Stepchildren and stepparents.* Unlike adopted children, stepchildren and stepparents are not counted for purposes of Section 318.
- *Brothers and sisters.*
- *Aunts and uncles.*
- *Nieces and nephews.*
- *Cousins.*
- *In-laws.*

✔ **Overlap in the Restricted Person Tests**   There will often be significant overlaps between the prohibited allocation rule applicable to selling shareholders and that applicable to more-than-25% shareholders, both as to the actual shareholders and as to their related parties. For example, if Father owned 50% of a company's outstanding stock and sold 30% to an ESOP and made the Section 1042 election, he would be a restricted person under both rules. However, if he did not make the Section 1042 rollover (but another shareholder did), he would still be a restricted person because of the more-than-25% shareholder rule. His children would also be considered more-than-25% shareholders because they would be considered to own any stock owned by their father. Accordingly, none of them could receive allocations attributable to Section 1042 employer securities from the ESOP.

It is therefore very important to examine both restricted person tests. An escape from one is not necessarily an escape from the other.

✔ **To What Allocations Does the Prohibited Allocation Rule Apply?**   The prohibited allocation rule does not prevent restricted persons from *participating* in an ESOP; it simply requires that no part of the plan's assets attributable to the 1042 stock be allocated, directly or indirectly, to a restricted person. Thus, plan assets other than Section 1042 stock (including employer stock contributed by the employer to the ESOP) can be allocated to a restricted person. However, the rule also prohibits "makeup" plan contributions for restricted persons. For example, if a restricted person were to receive an allocation of cash in an ESOP proportionate to the Section 1042 stock allocations received by the other participants, there would be an outright violation of the prohibited allocation rule. The legislative history states that the rule extends to all other qualified plans maintained by the ESOP sponsor, so that an employer could not make an allocation of other assets to a restricted person without making additional allocations to other participants sufficient to separately satisfy the nondiscrimination requirements of Section 401(a).[38]

The prohibited allocation rule is not applicable to amounts payable under a *non-qualified* deferred compensation arrangement, such as a stock option plan, a SERP, or a deferred compensation arrangement paid under a rabbi trust or otherwise.[39] However, if the employer corporation made the S election after the sale by a restricted person, deferred compensation would have to be examined in light of the nonallocation rule of Section 409(p).

Exceptions to the Prohibited Allocation Rule

✔ **De Minimis Exception for Lineal Descendants** There is a de minimis exception to the prohibited allocation rule for certain individuals who are restricted persons by virtue of being lineal descendants of a selling shareholder. Lineal descendants of a selling shareholder are allowed to receive allocations attributable to (or allocated in lieu of) employer securities sold in a Section 1042 sale where the aggregate amount allocated to all lineal descendants of a selling shareholder does not exceed more than 5% of the employer securities held by the plan that are attributable to Section 1042 sales by persons related to the lineal descendants. Relatedness for this purpose is determined by the same Section 267(c)(4) relatedness test used for the prohibited allocation rule. Because of the absolute 5% cap, any increase in the number of lineal descendants who participate in the ESOP will shrink the permissible per-participant allocation that can be made within the overall 5% exception.

Note: There is no similar exception for persons who are constructive more-than-25% shareholders because of attribution from related shareholders, so the de minimis exception will almost always be overridden by the more-than-25% shareholder rule.[40]

✔ **Shares Other Than the Section 1042 Shares** As noted above, shares purchased by an ESOP, but as to which no Section 1042 election has been made, are not subject to the prohibited allocation rule. So, for example, if three $33\frac{1}{3}$% shareholders each sell their employer securities to an ESOP, but only two of them elect the Section 1042 rollover, children of the electing shareholders (even though they are constructive more-than-25% shareholders) may receive allocations attributable to the shares purchased from the non-electing shareholder.[41]

✔ **Section 1042 Securities That Have Been Repurchased** The IRS has also ruled privately that Section 1042 employer securities previously allocated to an ESOP participant that have again become available for allocation after being repurchased from the ESOP participant on termination can be allocated to a constructive more-than-25% shareholder without violating the prohibited allocation rule.[42] The apparent theory of this ruling is that the shares were not "acquired by the plan . . . in a sale to which section 1042 applies."[43] Under this rationale, any restricted person could receive an allocation of employer securities so long as the shares had been "purged" by having been distributed and reacquired by the ESOP in a sale to which Section 1042 did not apply. This would not be the case with unvested shares that were forfeited and reallocated to a restricted person.

How Long Does the Prohibited Allocation Rule Apply?

In the case of a selling shareholder or related person, there is a 10-year nonallocation period during which the prohibited allocation rule applies. If the stock sale in question was financed with a loan that is outstanding for more than 10 years from the stock acquisition date, the nonallocation period is extended until the final ESOP plan allocation is made when the loan is paid off.[44]

In the case of an actual or constructive more-than-25% shareholder at the time the 1042 securities are sold to the ESOP, or during the prior one-year period, the restriction lasts until all of the employer securities acquired in the sale are allocated.[45] In the case of a person who is not a more-than-25% shareholder at the time of the 1042 sale to the ESOP but later becomes one, only stock ownership on the date ESOP shares are allocated is counted.[46]

Consequences of Not Meeting the Rule

✔ **Disqualification as to the Restricted Person** If an ESOP fails to comply with the prohibited allocation rule and makes an allocation to a restricted person, Section 409(n) in effect treats the ESOP as being disqualified, but only with respect to the restricted person.[47] The restricted person is treated as having received a taxable distribution from the ESOP equal to the allocation. If the restricted person has not attained age 59½, the excise tax on premature distributions will also be applicable.

Because the prohibited allocation is unlikely to be accompanied by an actual distribution from the ESOP that could help meet the resulting tax obligations, a compliance failure will be doubly burdensome to the restricted person affected.

✔ **Fifty Percent Excise Tax on Employer** The employer sponsoring the ESOP (or the worker-owned cooperative that consented to the Section 1042 rollover) also bears the brunt of a failure to comply with the prohibited allocation rule in the form of a 50% excise tax on the amount of the prohibited allocation.[48]

Conclusion

Especially during the first ESOP plan year following a stock purchase and Section 1042 rollover, the employer and plan administrator must be wary of the prohibited allocation rule. It is important to examine the related party attribution rules of Section 267 and the constructive ownership rules of Section 318 to determine which ESOP participants, in addition to the selling shareholder and more-than-25% shareholders, might be affected by the prohibited allocation rule. In plan years thereafter, attention must be paid to whether any participant has *become* a more-than-25% shareholder to whom the prohibited allocation rule applies.

NOTES

1. Section 1042 permits a C corporation shareholder to sell his or her shares to an ESOP that will own 30% or more of the corporation's stock after the sale and to reinvest the proceeds without recognizing a current gain on the sale for tax purposes.

2. References to ESOPs should be understood to include eligible worker-owned cooperatives.

3. Code § 409(n)(1).

4. Private Letter Ruling (PLR) 9041071 (July 18, 1990).

5. Although Temp. Treas. Reg. § 1.1042-1T A-2(a)(3)(ii) limits the prohibited allocation rule to family members under Code § 267(c)(4), the applicable provision in § 409(n)(1)(A)(ii) imposes the rule on a broader range of related persons. This follows from an amendment to the restricted allocation rule in the 1986 Tax Reform Act that is not reflected in the regulation.

6. See Code § 409(n)(1)(A)(ii).

7. Code § 267(c)(4).

8. Treas. Reg. §1.267(C)-1(a)(4).

9. See PLR 9143013 (October 25, 1991).

10. A trust grantor and beneficiary are not considered related parties for this purpose. There are a number of other fiduciary relationships specified in Code § 267(b), but they should not be applicable in the context of the prohibited allocation rule. For example, the fiduciary (i.e. trustee) and grantor of a trust, and the trustees of related trusts, are considered related parties for purposes of § 267(b). Under § 267, this prevents a grantor from recognizing a loss upon transferring property to his or her own trust and prevents related trusts from shuffling assets back and forth to create paper losses. However, the IRS ruled in PLR 9017008 that where the grantor and trustee are acting for their own accounts (e.g., where the trustee is receiving the property in his or her own name rather than for the trust), as would be the case in an ESOP allocation, § 267(b) does not apply. See also Rev. Rul. 59-171, 1959-1 C.B. 65.

11. PLR 9508001 (October 13, 1994).

12. Under Code § 267(c)(1), for purposes of applying § 267(b), stock owned by a partnership is considered owned proportionately by its partners. Under § 267(c)(5), stock owned by a partnership and attributed to a partner is considered actually owned by the partner and is attributed to the partner's family members.

13. Rev. Rul. 59-43, 1959-1 C.B. 146. This ruling was based on the identical definition of an individual's "family" for personal holding company purposes in Code § 544(a)(2).

14. *Tilles v. Comm'r*, 38 BTA 545 (1938), *aff'd*, 113 F.2d 907 (8th Cir.), *cert. denied*, 311 U.S. 703 (1940).

15. Rev. Rul. 71-50, 1971-1 C.B. 106.

16. Id.

17. *Stern v. Comm'r*, 215 F.2d 701 (3d Cir. 1954).

18. A controlled group for this purpose is defined in Code § 409(l)(4), which generally requires 50% parent-subsidiary ownership.

19. Code § 409(n)(3)(B)(i).

20. See § 318(a)(1)(B).

21. Code § 318(a)(2)(A).

22. Code §§ 318(a)(3)(A), 318(a)(5)(C).

23. Code § 318(a)(5)(E).

24. Code § 318(a)(2)(A).

25. Treas. Reg. § 1.318-3(a).

26. As with partnerships, although stock owned by a beneficiary is considered to be owned by the estate, this does not cause the beneficiaries to be considered to own each other's holdings. See Code § 318(a)(5)(C).

27. Code § 318(a)(2)(B)(i).

28. Treas. Reg. § 20.2031-7. See Treas. Reg. § 1.318-3(B).

29. Code § 318(a)(2)(B)(ii).

30. Code § 409(n)(1) (flush language) provides that the employee trust exception of § 318(a)(2)(B)(i) does not apply for purposes of the prohibited allocation rule.

31. Senate Explanation, 1986 Tax Reform Act, Pub. L. No. 99-514 (October 22, 1986).

32. Code § 318(a)(2)(C).

33. Code § 318(a)(2)(C).

34. Code § 318(a)(4).

35. Rev. Rul. 68-601, 1968-2 C.B. 124.

36. Treas. Reg. § 1.318-1(b)(2).

37. See Treas. Reg. § 1.318-2(b).

38. Senate Explanation, 1986 Tax Reform Act, Pub. L. No. 99-514 (October 22, 1986).

39. Conference Report, 1986 Tax Reform Act, Pub. L. No. 99-514 (October 22, 1986); PLR 9442015 (October 21, 1994).

40. Given the 30% shareholding requirement of § 1042, a selling shareholder will always meet the test to be considered a more-

than-25% shareholder, unless smaller shareholders aggregate their stock sales to meet the 30% test. Such a selling shareholder's lineal descendants will consequently be constructive more-than-25% shareholders under the attribution rules of Code § 318. The IRS has confirmed that in its view, the lineal descendant exception is effectively meaningless (except for 25%-or-less shareholders who aggregate sales to an ESOP) because it does not convey protection from the more-than-25% shareholder rule. PLR 9707015 (November 14, 1996).

41. PLR 9001035 (October 10, 1989).

42. PLR 9001035 (October 10, 1989).

43. Code § 409(n)(1).

44. Code § 409(n)(3)(C).

45. Senate Explanation, 1986 Tax Reform Act, Pub. L. No. 99-514 (October 22, 1986).

46. Id.

47. Id.

48. Code § 4979A.

15

REINVESTING THE SECTION 1042 ROLLOVER

JAMES H. WILLIS
MICHAEL A. COFFEY

If you *sold* stock in a private company before 1984, you had little choice: take the proceeds and pay the capital gains taxes. However, you could *swap* your shares (if they constituted at least 80% of the company) for the stock of another private or public company and pay no taxes as long as you held the new shares. Section 1042 of the Internal Revenue Code (the Code), added by the Tax Reform Act of 1984, built on this second option to provide an attractive third alternative: Sell your shares to an ESOP, in any amount as long as the ESOP ends up with at least 30% of the company's equity, and pay no taxes provided you purchase and hold "qualified replacement property" (QRP), and the legal and procedural rules described earlier in this book are met.[1]

What Constitutes Qualified Replacement Property

QRP consists of securities of U.S. domestic operating corporations. More than 50% of the corporation's assets must be used in the active conduct of a business, and no more than 25% of gross income can be derived from passive sources.[2]

QRP includes U.S. stocks, bonds, debentures, other certificates of indebtedness, and convertibles, if they are securities of companies incorporated in the U.S. QRP does *not* include U.S. government and municipal bonds, mutual funds, and real estate investment trusts (REITs), or ownership of companies through vehicles other than securities (e.g., a partnership interest).

✔ **Factors Bearing on QRP Status**   The process is hardly as simple as the above lists might indicate. For example, bank stocks are qualified, being specifically exempted from the passive income rule. Other securities might require a special ruling. Is a Tennessee Valley Authority bond clearly an ineligible governmental security? With a variety of noncallable, high-grade corporate bonds rated A or better and having 30 years to maturity, why test a gray area when there is no meaningful difference in the return on investment? Note also that convertible securities are valid for the rollover so long as (1) they are convertible into acceptable properties and (2) conversion was a part of the security when originally issued. The conversion is not a taxable event, nor is the gift of QRP to someone else, to a charity, or to certain trusts. A sale for cash does unleash tax on the capital gain.[3] Additionally, the maturity or call of a bond triggers taxation; care must be taken to analyze any prospectus so as to avoid amortizing or sinking fund debentures, or escape the pitfall of brokers and traders who do not fully understand the ESOP rollover.

Some additional confusion may arise at times from public issuers of "ESOP" securities. These are not necessarily QRP candidates, but merely securities coming from an ESOP sponsored by the issuing corporation, e.g. the Procter & Gamble ESOP bonds from the P&G employee trust (the difficulty with these is the presence of a sinking fund that can trigger a taxable event in a rollover portfolio). Also, ownership by a foreign corporation (not a foreign individual) may be a disqualifying factor and not readily apparent.

The purchased replacement securities can also be those of a private corporation meeting the rollover criteria, even (under certain circumstances) a company owned by the selling shareholder. In this case, however, the investment goals should be clearly drawn. There are other ways to move proceeds from an ESOP sale into another private corporation, and the direct use of the "rollover" monies is not always the best. This is but one example among many where the structures of the rollover portfolio and the ESOP transaction are more closely linked than is commonly thought.

Another instance when the seller must be aware of this linkage is the collateralization of the ESOP loan with some or all of the replacement properties. It is helpful to have investment counsel knowledgeable in ESOP transactions brought into the decision-making processes early on.

Investor Objectives

In most cases, selling shareholders look for the following results:

- Never pay taxes on the ESOP sale proceeds.
- Preserve the capital base.
- Establish a high, stable current income from the rollover portfolio.
- Achieve some growth in this income over time to compensate for inflation.
- Increase the capital base.

Not every investor shares all of these objectives or places them in this order, but most ESOP reinvestors draw up a similar list in discussions of their goals. How do these affect the two major reinvestment decisions: (1) asset allocation and (2) portfolio structure (margined or no-loan)? How are they affected by the ESOP transaction design?

✔ **Asset Allocation** The typical requirement of some salary replacement for the seller often necessitates a bond component in the portfolio, in addition to some equities to provide for income growth. This asset mix varies from 50/50 stocks and bonds to 100% of either, depending on income objectives, risk tolerance, asset allocation outside the ESOP rollover investments, and, to a lesser extent, the timing of the purchases.

The tradeoff between the growth of income and the amount of current income is essentially the stocks versus bonds decision. The greater the proportional weight of stocks, the lower the current income, but the future income and growth of capital should be greater. This balance is roughly illustrated by table 15-1. The determination of the quantitative asset mix is one of the easier problems facing the investor. The yields of the various classes of securities are known and the investor knows generally the income he or she wants to derive from the holdings. There is obviously a conflict between growth and current income. You cannot have your cake and eat it too in this respect; the high growth and considerable current income the closely held company owner enjoyed before the sale usually cannot be duplicated with publicly traded securities. Most successful closely held business owners have reaped returns from their companies well over the 10% total return produced by broadly held company stocks.

Table 15-1. Asset Allocation

% in Bonds (6.5% Yield)	% in Stocks (1.5% Yield)	Current Yield on Total Account	Growth in Value of Portfolio & Income
0%	100%	1.5%	10%
20%	80%	2.5%	8%
40%	60%	3.5%	6%
60%	40%	4.5%	4%
80%	20%	5.5%	2%
100%	0%	6.5%	0%

Once the overall yield is decided, for example, $50,000 annually or 5% on a $1 million portfolio, we know that the stock-to-bond ratio in today's market will be about 40/60. This will also produce a compound growth of about 4% annually in the value of the portfolio, a bit better than the long-term rate of inflation (3.1% compounded since 1925).

Without elaborating on the kinds and quality of securities to be examined, we will note only that the securities selection on the equity side enjoys a much larger universe of candidates from which to choose than is the case for the income component, the bonds. In any case, an original prospectus should always be examined to determine the suitability of any issue.

The long-term decline in interest rates, in place since 1982, continues. This downtrend is in fact a long-term correction of the anomalously high rates of the 1970s and 1980s. Short of a return to these multi-year interest rate increases, bonds should be good vehicles for income purposes.

A very long-term view of interest rates is often of little interest to investors, who usually work with a time horizon of a year or less. The ESOP investor needs to understand the probable outcome of investing for interest income over much longer terms: 10, 20, or more years.

Still, a common question arising in the securities selection process is "What if I change my mind?" This is important, even though conservative investors have historically been best served by not changing their minds, but instead purchasing diversified quality in terms of earnings, stability, and immunity to obsolescence of the target company and then holding that quality for the long term (as they did holding their private company stock before the sale to the ESOP).

If the selling shareholder needs investments that can be changed without tax consequences, there are some useful techniques, though each has shortcomings that must be considered along with its advantages.

Investment Options

✔ **The Charitable Remainder Trust**   One way of creating a manageable portfolio with highly favored tax treatment is to establish a charitable remainder trust benefiting a tax-exempt organization, funded with some of the rollover stock (QRP).[4] This can be done at any time. The trust money can then be managed for any objective, typically to generate current income. The donor escapes capital gains and estate taxation while receiving income from the trust.

Additionally, the earnings coming to the donor from the charitable trust enjoy some income tax relief, though this benefit is, as a rule, much smaller than for direct gift deductions and is dependent upon the type of trust, the age of the donor(s), and the tax status of the donor. This income flows through to the donor(s) and designated beneficiaries until their deaths or some other time limit specified by the donor as allowed by law.

Of the principal types of such trusts, charitable remainder unitrusts (CRUTs) and charitable annuity trusts are the most common. The CRUT is most often the vehicle of choice in the ESOP environment. The donor gives appreciated property to a CRUT and retains the right to income from the trust for his or her life and/or that of the donor's spouse or for a fixed period. A donor further receives an income tax deduction for the net present value of the gift; this deduction is dependent on age and a percentage payout from the trust. It is always important to coordinate the ESOP investment choices with the overall estate plan.

Note that the private company stock itself could be contributed directly to a charity or to a charitable remainder unitrust as another piece of the ESOP perpetuation transaction. This would reduce the size of the estate (and estate taxes) and provide a tax shelter for current income. When redeemed later by the corporation, shareholders, or even the ESOP from the charitable unitrust, any resulting liquidity in the corpus of the CRUT could produce earnings for the selling shareholder (which private, non-dividend paying shares could not). The stock price may also be favorable for the buyers, whether the shares come directly from the charity or from a CRUT. The price may be affected by a lack-of-marketability discount, which could be helpful or disadvantageous, depending on the transaction goal.

The use of a variable annuity in the charitable trust can allow the payout from the CRUT to the donor to be built pretty much as the donor desires, at times with a much greater income to the donor later. Also, this may be an appealing way to do less than a 30% ESOP, increase net after-tax income to the seller, and avoid the attribution rules that otherwise affect allocations of ESOP shares, thus allowing the seller and his family to participate in the ESOP.

A drawback is that the donated principal, albeit manageable without taxation and yielding income to the donor on a tax-favored basis, is now irrevocably committed to the charity. The CRUT will be helpful as both the seller and the portfolio age, in that positions in a long-term portfolio can be converted to tax shields (against capital gains, estate, and income taxation) and high current income sources. It is not an appropriate way to treat all of one's private shares or rollover money, but can be quite powerful as a source of income and estate tax relief.

✔ **The Floating Rate Note**   After the rollover is taken, transactions in the replacement properties trigger taxation on the properties involved. Why not invest the rollover proceeds in a portfolio that is fixed in value and then borrow against the portfolio to produce manageable investments? Usually, up to 50% (more for certain bonds) of any portfolio can be margined, i.e. provide the support for a loan. This floating rate technique circumvents the conventional 50% constraint without risking a margin call.

The rollover proceeds are used to purchase a note maturing in 30 to 40 years, typically callable in 20 to 30 years. It operates much as a money market instrument does and yields about a third of a point less than commercial paper; e.g. if the commercial paper rate is 4%, then the principal base of the floating rate note will yield about 3.7%. The rate generally changes once a month. This rate adjustment provides for a stable principal amount for the security underpinning the loan. Now, up to 75% or more of the portfolio can be borrowed, with the borrowed monies to be invested without the "qualified property" limitations.

The lower rate on the total investment in the floating rate security generates the interest income to pay the higher loan interest on the borrowed funds. The spread between what interest is paid and what is earned may be positive or negative, depending on the changing market conditions. With today's lower interest rates, the resulting negative carry for such arrangements plus the additional "active" management fees can be drawbacks.

The spread between the two rates generally varies in a range of 30 to 300 basis points. As of this writing, the interest earned is roughly 5.7% and the interest paid on the borrowed funds is 8.0%, representing a larger spread of 230 basis points, for which the net earnings of the portfolio are low.

The floating rate note pays about 30 basis points less than the A1 P1 commercial paper rate, so the gap is approximately 2.6% as of this writing.

The interest rate forecast is an especially important key to the investment decision (as generally with all investing). In the declining rate environment we have experienced since 1982, the floating rate note will underperform fixed-rate bonds. If the very long-term forecast should envision sustained interest rate increases, the floating rate note should certainly be on the short list of investor options.

Before making this move, it is also important to understand the effect of portfolio changes: What does it truly cost to sell a position in a low-basis ESOP rollover portfolio? While the fully invested portfolio provides for more working capital than its margined counterpart for the ESOP reinvestment, some will ask, "What if there is an unforeseen taxable event in my portfolio?" Let us assume the worst case of no taxable basis in the forced change of position (table 15-2).

Table 15-2. The Effect of Portfolio Changes

Assume a $1 million ESOP rollover; a zero basis in all 25 positions, each of which starts at $40,000; and combined state and federal capital gains taxes of 25%.

Value of position	$ 40,000
Capital gains tax on forced sale	– 10,000
Net reinvested amount after taxes	30,000
Total resulting value of portfolio	990,000
Previous value of portfolio	1,000,000
Difference in value	$ 10,000
Difference as a percentage of total value	1.00%

If a change proves necessary or desirable, the replacement of a few positions among 30 or more over time should not present a significant taxation problem. Be sure the tax problem and the anticipated gains from active management are sufficient to offset the loss of effective capital. Note that if the capital gains tax rate is lowered, the effect of changes is reduced even more.

Because not all of the total sale proceeds are used, the margined portfolio will have to perform about 33% better than the standard portfolio to break even in terms of current income. Many elaborate models can be developed, but with any significant current income requirement, the loss of use of all the capital base that generates the earnings and the negative carry present a real handicap. Note that the returns are before management and ongoing brokerage fees, which in the actively managed case can be 1% or more of the managed asset value. This further reduces net income available to the investor.

The principal use of the floating rate note is to produce growth of portfolio value. The central intention is for the performance of the actively managed securities purchased on margin to outstrip that of the "passive" 100%. At some point the performance of this investment option should be significantly ahead of its passive counterpart (otherwise, why do it?). This is true when there is a long enough run for the invested margined portfolio, growing at an assumed faster rate, to outgrow the handicaps mentioned above. How long is this run?

Assume that the rollover proceeds are fully invested in equities. If the actively managed equities are assumed to outperform the passive portfolio stocks by 20%, the managed equity value could just catch up to the "passive" equity in about 15 years.

For the younger investor who wishes to delay current income and can grow value through active management, this approach could make a lot of sense. This is even more true if there is a desire to direct some of the assets into another private corporation or venture that is riskier, but hopefully much more rewarding than the public markets.

This typically younger investor would want to be comfortable with some simple issues:

• Will the investment adviser really sustain a consistent 20% or greater advantage over the buy-and-hold portfolio in the long run? It is often quite useful to talk with other individual investors about their experience with active management versus holding quality securities for the long term.

- Is it really necessary to margin 75% or 80% or more of the aggregate proceeds? Recall that about 50% of a conventional portfolio (built around securities with yields higher than the money market rates of floating rate notes) can be margined to produce flexibility for risk taking.

One final point about floating rate notes: With this strategy, the QRP (the money market instrument) is a debt security of only one or a very few, but very large companies. It could be questioned whether this represents portfolio strength through diversification.

✔ **Annuitization**   This is the you-can-always-spend-it approach. The availability of a liquid block of capital to the investor opens up the possibility of considering the gradual attrition of some portion of the principal as part of the income payout. The reasons are as different as the investors themselves, though the process essentially includes two steps: (1) conservatively identify the base principal amount needed for security with advancing years and (2) ascertain the average annual income wanted in the more active years.

A $1,000,000 rollover fully invested for growth (assuming a 10% annual increase) and earning 2.5% or $25,000 yearly could be made to yield a total income of $50,000 by accepting less growth (about 7.5% annually). Such payouts can be advantageous by (1) resulting in capital gains tax as opposed to income taxation, (2) reducing the size of the taxable estate (about 55% for many estates), and (3) making income entirely at the discretion of the investor.

At death, the rollover properties go to the estate with the stepped-up basis. Though there are no capital gains ever paid, there are estate taxes, at least on the money that did not get spent. These taxes for heirs are often 50%-plus. Whether building a "self-funded annuity," using some life insurance funding for the estate, or using a charitable trust, there is a lot to consider. Be sure that your advisers have looked at all options; sometimes an attractive alternative is never even brought to the table.

✔ **What Else Can I Do?**   Whatever is done, the question to ask is: "Is this strategy appropriate to the investor?" Most

ESOP transactions do not involve tens of millions of dollars. An ESOP Association survey reported 86 transactions with a total volume of $490 million. Only about half took advantage of the Section 1042 rollover: (1) 50% of the transactions were $2 million or less, (2) 80% of the transactions were $6 million or less, and (3) 10% of the transactions were over $10 million. This small statistical sample is representative of what we find in our experience nationally.

Appropriate to larger amounts are some less frequently encountered strategies that entail greater complexity and risk. The financial economy of scale makes the higher transaction costs of these techniques less important, while providing the typically younger investor with flexibility for predominantly equity investing.

Ideas that are beyond the scope of this short chapter, but should be investigated by the relatively small number of ESOP investors with larger amounts, include (1) a perpetual short against the box; (2) "deep in the money" calls; (3) equity swaps; (4) zero-cost dollars; and (5) invest in NewCo, Inc.

The underlying concept for the first four of these techniques is analogous to the floating rate note: identify an investment as the QRP that can be "stabilized" in some fashion, then borrow against that "stabilized" investment to produce what are essentially loan proceeds free of the tax constraints. If the fees and carrying costs are offset by the performance of the smaller amount of capital, then the program can make numerical sense.

The last strategy on the list (though probably not the last we will hear of, given the inventiveness of the financial community) is "Invest in NewCo": a new operating (closely held) company meeting the requirements of Section 1042 is designated as the QRP. Such a strategy appears to technically qualify so long as at least 50%-plus of the assets are involved in the active conduct of a trade or business. The remaining 49% or less is then operated as a closed-end investment company for actively trading in the securities markets without tax penalties.

What the NewCo investor has achieved is the movement of capital from one operating company to another, with the attendant exposure to the risks of the new private company—or at least 50% of the private company. A central issue is whether this truly represents the diversification and simplification ESOP investors generally seek. Those familiar with the psychological profile of such investors recognize that they have usually taken a lifetime of risk meeting payrolls, covering loans, and dealing with the many issues in running a corporation. Most rollover investors are looking for an environment to reduce both risk and worry.

The younger investor with a profitable corporation capable of sustaining an ESOP buyout for the NewCo strategy might be better served by a Section 368 non-taxable exchange with NewCo or the direct use of the existing corporation's cash flow.

A more general concern than just the financial performance of these packages is the potential treatment of high levels of "margining" by the IRS. At what point does the economic substance of the transaction, regardless of the technical justification for the intervening steps, really represent a taxable disposition of the QRP? Again, the more risk-tolerant investor with larger amounts should talk to a number of expert practitioners to get some measure of the true risk/reward (in all senses) of a particular strategy.

Conclusion

Ongoing exposure to corporate risks should carry appropriate rewards. The selling shareholder may want to stagger the sales of stock to better participate in the growth of the company while phasing out his or her ownership. This would also enable the dollar-cost averaging of the acquisition of the replacement properties, a potentially very helpful approach that could considerably widen the sometimes limiting one-year reinvestment window by creating a sequence of "windows of opportunity."

Another consideration is control. Since the availability of the 1042 tax-deferred rollover requires consent from the corporation, would the company provide this consent once control was relinquished? Remember too that the ESOP cannot be committed beforehand to any stock purchases; they must be in the best interests of the plan participants as decided by the trustee. Those interests can change with the fortunes of the sponsoring corporation.

If the replacement properties are to provide some collateral for the ESOP loan, the lender and the investment adviser should at least have a conversation concerning the appropriate securities for this. It has been said that occasionally some lenders are more comfortable with the "money market" type of securities underlying a floating rate note. This is generally a misperception by the lender, because high quality corporate issues are quite adequate. The reinvestor should build the portfolio based on his or her needs, not somebody else's wants. As seen elsewhere in this chapter, this is just one of many areas open to negotiation where advisors are helpful.

Be very clear about needs and objectives. If the private company is returning a high level of compensation, it might make more sense to delay the rollover. It is sometimes the case that the value of the compensation stream (even in terms of the "net present value") is much greater than the amount that can be realized from an ESOP stock sale.

You might be better served to pre-fund the ESOP (taking advantage of pretax contributions and compounding) for a later stock purchase with less leverage on the company, depending on your assessment of the company strength and the effect of possible leveraged sales on value.

Most rollover investors are looking for safety and earnings. They have borrowed money most of their business lives to operate their company and look forward to a time with minimal complexity and debt. A stable, fully invested portfolio will frequently answer most of these needs, although some form of charitable trust could be considered if (1) there is a clearly identifiable block of principal that will never be needed as a liquid asset; (2) estate taxes are to be reduced; and (3) the age, income concerns, and philanthropic goals of the investor are compatible with the strategy.

Remember that rollover reinvesting is not done in isolation and that at a minimum, the investment strategy should be linked to other key elements: (1) the treatment of other investment assets, such as pension funds, inheritances, and savings; (2) the overall business succession plan, which can affect the value of remaining closely held shares; (3) the ESOP transaction design; and (4) the seller's estate plan. In all of the possible ESOP rollover variations, there are no universally perfect investment ideas. There is generally, however, an investment strategy that fits the unique needs of each investor.

NOTES

1. For example, see the chapter "An Introduction to Section 1042."
2. Code § 1042(c)(4)(B)(ii).
3. Code § 1042(e)(3).
4. See PLR 9234023 (May 26, 1992), which states, as would be expected, that there is no recognition of taxable gain for the contribution of QRP to a CRUT.

Appendix 15-1: Sample Statement of Election

STATEMENT OF ELECTION

I hereby irrevocably elect nonrecognition treatment under Section 1042(a) of the Internal Revenue Code of 1986 with respect to the sale of the following qualified securities:

1. ___ shares of voting common stock ("Shares") of _____.

                                                      (Company)

2. Date of sale of the Shares: _____, 20____.

3. Adjusted basis of the Shares: $_____.

4. Amount realized upon the sale of the Shares: $_____.

5. The Shares were sold to the _____ Employee Stock Ownership Plan.

    I have attached to this Statement of Election a verified Statement of Consent executed by the _____ of the Company.

_____

Signature of the Seller

_____

Tax I.D. Number

Appendix 15-2: Sample Statement of Consent

STATEMENT OF CONSENT

In connection with the sale of shares of the common stock of

_____,
(Company)

by _____ to the

_____ Employee Stock Ownership Plan,
the Company hereby consents to the application of Sections 4978
and 4979A of the Internal Revenue Code of 1986.

Date: _____   By _____

                                      Title _____

VERIFICATION

I hereby declare under penalties of perjury that I am the duly
elected _____ of _____,
that I have read the foregoing Statement of Consent, and that to
the best of my knowledge and belief such Statement is true and
correct.

Date: _____

Appendix 15-3: Sample Statement of Purchase

STATEMENT OF PURCHASE

I hereby declare that the securities described below constitute the "qualified replacement property" with respect to the sale of qualified securities under Section 1042 of the Internal Revenue Code of 1986.

DESCRIPTION   NUMBER   NET COST   DATE PURCHASED

Date: _____

State of _____)
) ss.
County of _____)

    I, _____, a notary public for the County aforesaid, in the State of _____, do certify that _____, whose name is signed to the writing above, bearing date on the ___ day of _____, 20__, has acknowledged the same before me in my County aforesaid.
    Given under my hand and official seal this ___ day of ____, 20__.
    My term of office expires on the ___ day of _____. 20__.

_____
Notary's Signature

(SEAL)

16

CASE STUDIES OF SECTION 1042 ROLLOVER REINVESTMENTS

JAMES H. WILLIS

Clearly, an initial goal for most owners considering selling to an ESOP and electing the rollover under Section 1042 of the Internal Revenue Code is to *never pay the taxes!* This attitude often moderates as the process unfolds to one of "let's postpone paying any capital gains taxes as long as possible, but consider changes when they are to my benefit from a long-term investment point of view."

Before discussing other common goals of sellers considering the Section 1042 rollover, it would be helpful to review the "population characteristics" of the Section 1042 rollover market. The Finance Advisory Committee of the ESOP Association has for several years conducted an informal survey of ESOP transactions. It might be surprising to some, but these surveys indicate that the Section 1042 rollover is used in only one-half to two-thirds of ESOP transactions. Further, 10% to 15% of Section 1042 transactions involve total sale proceeds of less than $500,000; approximately half are for less than $2 million, and two-thirds to three-quarters are for less than $6 million. Lastly, it is quite common for the sales proceeds from a transaction to be divided among a number of owners, making the apparent $5 million transaction really five individual $1 million transactions. A seller with $25 million to invest can consider techniques that might not be appropriate for someone with $1 million. The dollars involved are obviously one of the more important factors conditioning the reinvestment strategy.

As one might expect, the most common age bracket for sellers considering a rollover is 55 to 70, where retirement and estate planning are beginning. However, because of gifts and inheritances, as well as the rapid growth of equity values created in newer fields such as computer and information technologies, sellers can be and are at times much younger. Age is another one of the major determinants of appropriate investment techniques.

For those who are in the retirement range, capital preservation is generally the number one goal; number two is current income (as a rollover investor remarked recently, "I don't have to try and make a fortune with these proceeds; I just don't want to lose what I have!"). Growth of principal and income also are important, but usually well below the first two objectives by a considerable amount. For the younger seller, the income requirement is often less important than the desire to grow principal (i.e., to continue to take risks).

Four Successful Case Studies

While a variety of investment strategies are available for those considering an ESOP rollover, sellers and their advisors should match the seller's needs and goals to the strategy chosen. The following cases outline the planning and execution of four actual Section 1042 rollover programs.

✔ **Case One: Mr. A** In 1989, Mr. A decided to make a partial sale to an ESOP of 30% of his stock in a closely held company he had founded in 1949 at age 19. Before the sale, he owned 100% of the outstanding stock. He was 59 at the time of the sale and planned to work "forever." His investment experience at that point was relatively limited, but he was eager to expand his knowledge as time permitted. His initial thought was to buy only stocks: "I have no need for income."

After extensive discussions, it was decided that a portfolio that was 75% in stocks and 25% in long-term, non-callable corporate bonds fit his needs. This mix would give him diversification not only among companies and industries, but also among security types. He could reinvest the bond income if not needed, and the quality, long-term fixed rate bonds would be an excellent "anchor to windward" in case of a severe economic downturn. He expressed no interest in a strategy of borrowing to create a portfolio that could be actively managed without high tax costs. Over the following 12 months a portfolio was constructed under these guidelines; some purchases were at his suggestion.

In 1993, Mr. A decided to make a second sale to the ESOP, this time taking the ESOP to a majority position. (In the intervening four years, the 1989 portfolio of qualified replacement properties had increased generally in line with the major market averages; no changes had been made in the holdings.) As expected, his thoughts about working forever also had changed. He had purchased a second home and was beginning to consider retiring. Income was now more important, and lengthy discussions were held on the pros and cons of bonds, utility stocks, and growth stocks; an equal portion of each was his eventual decision. His interest in the market had also increased, as had his desire to help choose the individual securities. As before, he expressed no interest in the various choices to borrow and reinvest the proceeds.

A third and final sale is planned in the next year or so, which will complete his transition from the only owner of a sizable closely held company, with all that entails, to a retired "investor."

The underlying portfolio chosen as "qualified replacement property" remains generally unchanged. He decided to sell two issues because they had risen rapidly and he felt they were "overpriced." In both cases, after an intermediate drop, the securities have again risen in value past the point where they were sold, and the government is happy to receive the tax proceeds! The income from the portfolio more than meets his needs, and his interest in managing this "excess" income for growth remains unabated. Had Mr. A even been able to execute the same sequence of sales with conventional corporate stock redemptions, the resulting portfolios would have been 30% below today's value, not to mention the after-tax costs to the company.

✔ **Case Two: Mr. and Mrs. B** In 1989, Mr. and Mrs. B decided to sell a majority interest in their company to an ESOP. The company had been in existence for about 10 years; their sons owned the remaining shares outside the ESOP and planned to remain with the company as management. The exclusion of the sons from ESOP allocations (under the Internal Revenue Code's prohibited allocation rule) was acceptable to all parties.

Mr. and Mrs. B were both about 50 years old and planned to use the proceeds from their sale to retire; therefore, income was very important to them. They both had limited experience with the public securities markets. After extensive discussion, they decided a portfolio of 75% long-term bonds and 25% growth stocks fit their needs.

The stocks in the rollover portfolio have done slightly better than the overall market since 1989. The bonds also have done well, because long-term interest rates have continued to fall. The income produced remains secure, but they recognize that the price increases in the bond portion are not likely to continue. There have been no changes in the qualified replacement securities since their purchase; a portion of the after-tax income produced by the rollover portfolio has been reinvested in other common stocks.

Recently their sons have considered selling the entire company to a publicly traded competitor for a substantial premium over the price paid by the ESOP in 1989. If that transaction were to occur at the anticipated price, and if Mr. and Mrs. B had retained their ownership and not sold to the ESOP, they would have more wealth from the process than with the ESOP (even after paying over $1 million of capital gains taxes). However, their decision to diversify at age 50 is one they continue to approve. They understood the risks of their closely held business and were content with the peace of mind resulting from the switch in their financial risk-versus-reward balance.

✔ **Case Three: Mr. C** In 1991 Mr. C sold 30% of his company to an ESOP; he continued to own the remaining 70%. The company had been in existence for about 10 years at the time and had experienced substantial growth. He was in his mid-50s and wished to create a diversified portfolio as a safety measure in case the company, which was heavily dependent on government contracts, did not continue its rapid rise. In his words, he wanted to "create a rock to stand on in a swamp" in case unforeseen trouble came. When business is going well, it is often hard to imagine such an occurrence. In fact, however, that is what happened. Within two years the company was sold to a larger competitor, and Mr. C received very little from the sale of his remaining shares.

The portfolio of qualified replacement securities that fit his needs contained 70% long-term bonds and 30% in growth stocks. There have been no changes in the portfolio since it was created and it has generally tracked with the major market averages. Because of income from other sources, he does not use all of the income produced, and has been reinvesting it in a separate portfolio.

From time to time he has made charitable gifts using the securities in the Section 1042 rollover portfolio. Because of their low tax basis, they make excellent charitable gifts. He receives a tax deduction based on the securities' value at the time of the gift, just as he would with a cash contribution. The charity sells the security and has its funds. The donor can keep the cash that would have been contributed and use it to invest without a low tax basis. He has used the securities purchased with the unneeded income, which have a much more up-to-date tax basis, to make gifts to children to avoid passing on to another generation the low tax basis of the qualified replacement property.

The seller has decided not to use any margin techniques in managing his securities portfolio. However, he has on several occasions borrowed against the holdings for short periods to purchase sailboats before selling the boat he owned at the time. Once the sale of the boat was completed, the margin debt was paid off.

✔ **Case Four: Mr. D** Mr. D. made the first of what is expected to be a series of sales to his company's ESOP in 1993. He and three partners owned all of the shares; all made equal sales to the ESOP in 1993 to bring the ESOP ownership to the 30%

threshold necessary for the Section 1042 rollover. If the decision to sell in 1993 had been Mr. D's alone, he would not have sold any shares at that time. He believes that the value of the closely held company stock will continue to rise at a much faster pace than shares in the public marketplace. Because of an internal agreement between the four owners, all four had to sell in the initial sale to the ESOP. Two older owners would then complete their sales while the two younger owners (including Mr. D) would wait.

Mr. D, who is in his late 40s, plans to work for another six to eight years and then retire. At that time he plans to have sold all of his shares to the ESOP. He wants "maximum income," not now but when he retires. A portfolio of bonds would have maximized income now but provided opportunity for little growth in principal and no growth in income. The income could be reinvested while it was not needed, but only after income taxes had been paid.

He decided to purchase a portfolio of growth stocks with dividends averaging about 2.0%—not much current income. However, the stocks were capable of growing and the dividends also could increase over time. Assuming conservative, long-term growth for stocks of about 10%, the portfolio could double in seven years, as could income. The principal growth also would be compounding untaxed. Mr. D has little experience with the stock market and little interest in acquiring such experience. Likewise, what reading he has done convinced him that buying strong companies and holding was a strategy that generally worked; it certainly had for him in his closely held company!

Additionally, if the income was not satisfactory at retirement, small sales of stock could be made to supplement the dividends. Income taxes would be due on the dividends as received (as high as 40% or more under existing tax laws); capital gains taxes would be due on any sales consummated (28% under current federal tax laws). The sales would be entirely voluntary. Mr. D briefly borrowed against his portfolio to purchase a second home before obtaining a mortgage. The margin loan was needed for less than a year and enabled him to negotiate an attractive cash price for the property. He is considering the possibility of contributing qualified replacement property to charities over time to re-place existing cash contributions.

Rescues and Near Misses in ESOP Rollover Transactions

The following is a short and far from exhaustive list of some near misses experienced by ESOP reinvestors.

✔ **Estate Planning** Based on normally sound estate planning counsel from their legal advisors, the clients were first told to transfer $1 million of *unreinvested* ESOP sale proceeds to their spouses. Because their spouses had not owned any of the shares sold to the ESOP, the spouses had no "rollover rights."

The sellers received the correct investment advice later not to transfer the unreinvested proceeds to their spouses. Each seller purchased $1 million in qualified replacement properties (in fact, they bought what their ineligible spouses directed). The replacement securities were then transferred into the name of the non-selling spouses, successfully completing both the rollover and the estate planning. If this advice had not been taken, more than a quarter of a million dollars in capital gains taxes would have been due in each transaction.

In another case, a seller knew he was terminally ill when the ESOP sale was planned. Before the sale, an investment program was prepared, which was implemented within days of the actual sale. Had he died during the reinvestment period, any qualified replacement property purchased before death would receive a step-up in basis. His estate could complete the rollover; however, any qualified replacement property bought after his death would retain the low tax basis from the original shares sold to the ESOP until the death of his beneficiaries. The seller did die early, but this problem was avoided for the beneficiaries.

✔ **When Does the Clock Start?** In many instances, sellers confuse the receipt of the sale proceeds as the beginning of their reinvestment period and their Statements of Election (to elect the Section 1042 rollover) so indicate. Reinvestment is allowed from 3 months before to 12 months after *the stock conveyance to the ESOP,* not the receipt of the proceeds. This discrepancy has been caught several times, in one case leaving only two days to successfully complete the rollover.

✔ **Look, Ma, No Filings!**   One group of sellers had been supplied with blank Statements of Election and Consent by their attorneys. These had apparently been lost in the closing paperwork late in December. They had asked their accountant about the necessary steps for IRS notification and were told that none were needed! A seemingly routine call from the investment advisor stopped the sellers from filing their tax returns without the needed ESOP filings—literally on the day the returns were to be mailed. This saved one-third of the proceeds from taxes.

✔ **What Did You Buy?**   Many prospective ESOP investors ask if mutual funds can constitute their qualified replacement property. While the answer is clearly no, this is not a problem because rollover investors will generally create their own diversified "mutual fund" by buying a portfolio of stocks and bonds suited to their needs. Many bonds are really amortizing debentures or have internal sinking funds—which render them callable and trigger taxation. It is possible to find solid, 30-year, non-callable bonds. A discipline of never committing to a purchase until an original prospectus is in hand for study has prevented many incorrectly and inaccurately described bonds from being purchased.

✔ **The Charitable Gift**   One seller called during the reinvestment period after the sale to say that he had just given a check for $250,000 to a charity. The check was drawn against the portion of the ESOP sale proceeds which had not yet been invested in qualified replacement property. The seller was strongly advised to retrieve the check from the charity and replace it with $250,000 of already purchased qualified replacement property. Otherwise, there would not be enough funds to complete the rollover, and capital gains taxes would be required.

The seller did recover the check at the last minute, invested the full amount of the sale in qualified replacement property and still made the charitable gift. The result was about $80,000 in capital gains tax savings, which otherwise would have been lost.

Conclusion

For the seller making a solitary sale to an ESOP and electing the Section 1042 rollover, the selections are of perhaps greater importance than for the seller who plans to sell in two, three, or more transactions. In Mr. D's case, he will likely have a variety of markets in which to decide, greater experience with the public markets based on previous sales, and perhaps a changed view of his long-term needs.

Selling shareholders also must examine their entire financial and estate situation when making plans for an ESOP rollover; they should not make the decisions in isolation. Long-term decisions can be successful if that is the horizon used when the decisions are made. Be aware that most investment counsel do not have extensive experience with Section 1042 transactions and consider investing for even a one-year time horizon a very long-term strategy indeed!

Understand the choices and risks, as well as your own needs and experience, before committing any funds to the process. Sometimes investors also hear that there is a single, scientific way to structure the rollover portfolio. Listening to experienced advice from both professionals and those who have actually traveled the trail ahead can be of inestimable value in making critical, often one-time decisions. There is no need to complete your ESOP sale successfully and then later worry about when you might have to "circle the wagons" to compensate for a deficient reinvestment strategy. The ESOP rollover has been pioneered by many investors since Section 1042 was enacted, and the successful strategies are well known.

ABOUT THE AUTHORS

Bruce F. Bickley is a senior vice president-Investments and senior portfolio manager-Portfolio Management Program for UBS Financial Services Inc. who specializes in working with selling shareholders in Section 1042 transactions. He is a CPA with a Masters of Taxation and frequently speaks on ESOPs throughout the United States.

Michael A. Coffey is a managing vice-president of Corporate Capital Resources responsible for structuring stock transactions and key executive benefit packages.

Donald Davis was formerly a managing director in the Global Corporate and Investment Banking group of Bank of America.

Ronald J. Gilbert is the cofounder and president of ESOP Services, Inc., in Scottsville, VA. With over 25 years of ESOP experience, he serves as a director of several ESOP companies and on the board of governors of the ESOP Association and is a coauthor of *Employee Stock Ownership Plans: Business Planning, Implementation, Law and Taxation*.

Douglas A. Jaques is a partner in the Los Angeles office of the law firm of McDermott, Will & Emery.

David R. Johanson is the managing attorney and counselor at law with Johanson Berenson LLP, which has offices in Napa, Pasadena, and San Francisco, California; Washington, D.C.; Arlington and Great Falls, Virginia; and Cary, North Carolina. His practice focuses on employee ownership, ESOPs, executive compensation (including various types of stock option plans), business succession and estate planning, general corporate matters, and various types of mergers and acquisitions transactions. Mr. Johanson is a member of the NCEO's board of directors and a member of the editorial board of the NCEO's *Journal of Employee Ownership Law and Finance.*

Joseph V. Rafferty is the managing director of Private Capital Corporation, a Northern California-based consulting firm serving ESOP companies for over 20 years. A specialist in broadened ownership strategies, he installs ESOPs across the country and is a frequent writer and speaker on the subject.

Scott Rodrick is the director of publishing and information technology at the National Center for Employee Ownership (NCEO). Mr. Rodrick created and maintains the NCEO's Web sites and is the author of the NCEO's booklet *An Introduction to ESOPs,* the editor and or/coauthor of various other NCEO publications, and the coeditor of *Employee Stock Ownership Plans* (Harcourt Brace, 1996, 1999). He served at the U.S. Department of Labor as an attorney-advisor before coming to the NCEO.

Corey Rosen is the NCEO's executive director and cofounder. He received his Ph.D. from Cornell University in political science in 1973, taught government at Ripon College until 1976, and then served as a Senate staff member until 1981, when he cofounded the NCEO. As a Senate staffer, he helped draft some of the current ESOP legislation. Mr. Rosen has coauthored four books and written over 100 articles on various aspects of employee ownership for a variety of professional, academic, and trade publications. He has lectured on the subject across the U.S. and abroad.

Robert F. Schatz is the founder and a partner in the West Hartford, Connecticut, law firm of Schatz Law Offices. His practice encompasses all aspects of employee ownership, particularly the design, negotiation, structuring, and implementation of ESOPs and ESOP stock purchase transactions. He provides legal advice to public and private corporations that sponsor or seek to establish an ESOP; to their shareholders, boards of directors, management, and employees; to ESOP fiduciaries; and to lending institutions and investors in ESOP financing transactions.

Brian Snarr is a partner at Morrison Cohen LLP in New York and is chair of the firm's Compensation and Benefits Practice Group. His practice includes advising employers, lenders, investors, and fiduciaries on the ERISA, tax, and business law aspects of employee compensation and benefit plans, as well as advising on the ERISA and benefits aspects of the firm's corporate, employment, and transactional practice areas. Mr. Snarr is active in private company ESOP structuring and finance, with substantial experience in the areas of tax and transactional structuring, corporate finance, and ERISA structuring and compliance. He is a member of various professional organizations, has lectured to legal and business audiences on ESOPs and other compensation and benefits topics, and has been quoted on ESOP matters in the business press. He received his B.A. from Haverford College in 1979 and his J.D. from the University of Virginia in 1982.

James G. Steiker is founder and a principal of Steiker, Fischer, Edwards & Greenapple, a law firm with offices in Philadelphia, Morristown, NJ, and Providence providing legal services to owners, employees, and trustees in connection with the creation, maintenance, and sale of employee-owned companies. He is also founder and principal of SES Advisors, Inc., which provides feasibility analyses and financial advisory services for ESOP transactions and plan administration services for ESOP companies.

James H. Willis is the president of Willis Investment Management Company, a national registered investment advisory firm located in Charlottesville, Virginia. He has a B.B.A. from the University of Georgia (Phi Beta Kappa) and an MBA from the University of Virginia. In addition, he is a Chartered Financial Analyst and a Chartered Investment Counselor. Before forming Willis Investment Management Company, Mr. Willis was a general partner and executive vice president at J & W Seligman & Company in New York City. He has spoken and written for many years on the subject of ESOP Section 1042 rollovers. ESOP rollover clients represent the majority of his firm's business.

ABOUT THE NCEO

The National Center for Employee Ownership (NCEO) is widely considered to be "the single best source of information on employee ownership anywhere in the world" (*Inc.* magazine, August 2000). Established in 1981 as a nonprofit information, research, and membership organization, it now has over 3,000 members, including companies, professionals, unions, government officials, academics, and interested individuals. It is funded entirely through the work it does.

The NCEO's mission is to provide the most objective, reliable information possible about employee ownership at the most affordable price possible. The NCEO publishes a variety of materials explaining how employee ownership plans work, describing how companies get employee owners more involved in making decisions about their work, and reviewing the research on employee ownership. In addition, the NCEO holds approximately 50 seminars, webinars, and conferences on employee ownership annually, and it offers a variety of online courses. The NCEO's work also includes extensive contacts with the media.

✔ **Membership Benefits**   NCEO members receive the following benefits (an introductory NCEO membership is $80; see the information on the following page):

- The bimonthly newsletter *Employee Ownership Report,* which covers ESOPs, stock options, and employee participation.

- Access to the members-only area of the NCEO Web site, including tools such as the NCEO's referral service, a searchable database of well over 200 service providers.

- Substantial discounts on publications and events produced by the NCEO (such as this book).

- The right to telephone or e-mail the NCEO for answers to general or specific questions regarding employee ownership.

NCEO Annual Membership Fees

An introductory NCEO membership costs $80 for one year ($90 outside the U.S.) and covers an entire company at all locations, a single person offering professional services in this field, or an individual with a business interest in employee ownership. Full-time students and faculty members who are not employed in the business sector may join at the academic rate of $35 for one year ($45 outside the U.S.). To join, see the order form at the end of this section, go to our Web site at *www.nceo.org,* or call us at (510) 208-1300 with your credit card in hand.

Selected NCEO Publications

The NCEO offers a variety of publications on all aspects of employee ownership and participation, from employee stock ownership plans (ESOPs) to stock options to employee participation. Below are descriptions of some of our main publications.

We publish new books and revise old ones on a yearly basis. To obtain the most current information on what we have available, visit our Web site at *www.nceo.org* or call us at 510-208-1300.

Employee Stock Ownership Plans (ESOPs)

- *The ESOP Reader* is an overview of the issues involved in establishing and operating an ESOP. It covers the basics of ESOP rules, feasibility, valuation, and other matters, and then discusses managing an ESOP company, including brief case studies. The book is intended for those with a general interest in ESOPs and employee participation.

   $25 for NCEO members, $35 for nonmembers

- This book, *Selling to an ESOP,* is a guide for owners, managers, and advisors of closely held businesses. It explains how ESOPs work and then offers a comprehensive look at legal structures, valuation, financing (including self-financing), and other matters, especially the tax-deferred section 1042 "rollover" that allows owners to indefinitely defer capital gains taxation on the proceeds of the sale to the ESOP.

$25 for NCEO members, $35 for nonmembers

- *Leveraged ESOPs and Employee Buyouts* discusses how ESOPs borrow money to buy out entire companies, purchase shares from a retiring owner, or finance new capital. Beginning with a primer on leveraged ESOPs and their uses, it then discusses contribution limits, valuation, accounting, feasibility studies, financing sources, and more.

  $25 for NCEO members, $35 for nonmembers

- The *Model ESOP* contains a sample ESOP plan, with alternative provisions given to tailor the plan to individual needs. It also includes a section-by-section explanation of the plan and other supporting materials.

  $50 for NCEO members, $75 for nonmembers

- *ESOP Valuation* brings together and updates where needed the best articles on ESOP valuation that we have published in our *Journal of Employee Ownership Law and Finance,* described below.

  $25 for NCEO members, $35 for nonmembers

- The *Employee Ownership Q&A Disk* gives Microsoft Windows users (any version from Windows 95 onward) searchable, point-and-click access to 500 questions and answers on all aspects of ESOPs.

  $75 for NCEO members, $100 for nonmembers

- *How ESOP Companies Handle the Repurchase Obligation* is a short publication with articles and research on the subject.

  $10 for NCEO members, $15 for nonmembers

- *The ESOP Committee Guide* describes the different types of ESOP committees, the range of goals they can address, alternative structures, member selection criteria, training, committee life cycle concerns, and other issues.

  $25 for NCEO members, $35 for nonmembers

- *Wealth and Income Consequences of Employee Ownership* is a detailed report on a comparative study of ESOP companies in Washington State that found ESOP companies pay more and provided better benefits than other companies.

  $10 for NCEO members, $15 for nonmembers

- *ESOPs and Corporate Governance* covers everything from shareholder rights to the impact of Sarbanes-Oxley to choosing a fiduciary.

  $25 for NCEO members, $35 for nonmembers

- *The ESOP Communications Sourcebook* provides ideas for and examples of communicating an ESOP to employees and customers. It includes a CD with communications materials, including many documents that readers can customize for their own companies.

  $35 for NCEO members, $50 for nonmembers

Stock Options and Related Plans

- *The Stock Options Book* is a straightforward, comprehensive overview covering the legal, accounting, regulatory, and design issues involved in implementing a stock option or stock purchase plan, including "broad-based" plans covering most or all employees. It is our main book on the subject and possibly the most popular book in the field.

  $25 for NCEO members, $35 for nonmembers

- *Selected Issues in Equity Compensation* is more detailed and specialized than *The Stock Options Book,* with chapters on issues such as repricing, securities issues, and evergreen options. The appendix is an exhaustive glossary of terms used in the field.

  $25 for NCEO members, $35 for nonmembers

- *Beyond Stock Options* is a guide to phantom stock, stock appreciation rights, restricted stock, direct stock purchase plans, and performance awards used as alternatives to stock options.

$35 for NCEO members, $50 for nonmembers

- *Accounting for Equity Compensation* is a guide to the financial accounting rules that govern equity compensation programs in the United States.

  $35 for NCEO members, $50 for nonmembers

- *Equity Compensation in a Post-Expensing World* is a collection of essays on strategies for choosing and structuring equity compensation plans when expensing is required.

  $25 for NCEO members, $35 for nonmembers

- *The Employee's Guide to Stock Options* is a guide for the everyday employee that explains in an easy-to-understand format what stock is and how stock options work.

  $25 for both NCEO members and nonmembers

- *Employee Stock Purchase Plans* covers how ESPPs work, tax and legal issues, administration, accounting, communicating the plan to employees, and research on what companies are doing with their plans. The book includes sample plan documents.

  $25 for NCEO members, $35 for nonmembers

- *Model Equity Compensation Plans* provides examples of incentive stock option, nonqualified stock option, and stock purchase plans, together with brief explanations of the main documents. A disk is included with copies of the plan documents in word processing formats.

  $50 for NCEO members, $75 for nonmembers

- *Current Practices in Stock Option Plan Design* reports on our survey of companies with broad-based stock option plans conducted in 2000. It includes a detailed examination of plan design, use, and experience broken down by industry, size, and other categories.

  $25 for NCEO members, $35 for nonmembers

- *Communicating Stock Options* offers practical ideas and information about how to explain stock options to a broad group of employees. It includes both essays and communication materials.

  $35 for NCEO members, $50 for nonmembers

- *Stock Options, Corporate Performance, and Organizational Change* presents the first serious research to examine the relationship between broadly granted stock options and company performance, and the extent of employee involvement in broad option companies.

  $15 for NCEO members, $25 for nonmembers

- *Equity-Based Compensation for Multinational Corporations* describes how companies can use stock options and other equity-based programs across the world to reward a global work force. It includes a country-by-country summary of tax and legal issues.

  $25 for NCEO members, $35 for nonmembers

- *Incentive Compensation and Employee Ownership* takes a broad look at how companies can use incentives, ranging from stock plans to cash bonuses to gainsharing, to motivate and reward employees. It includes both technical discussions and case studies.

  $25 for NCEO members, $35 for nonmembers

- *Tax and Securities Sources for Equity Compensation* is a compilation of statutory and regulatory material relevant to the study of equity compensation.

  $35 for NCEO members, $50 for nonmembers

Employee Involvement and Management

- *Ownership Management* draws upon the experience of the NCEO and of leading employee ownership companies to discuss how to build a culture of lasting innovation by combining employee ownership with employee involvement.

  $25 for NCEO members, $35 for nonmembers

Other

- *Section 401(k) Plans and Employee Ownership* focuses on how company stock is used in 401(k) plans, both in stand-alone 401(k) plans and combination 401(k)–ESOP plans ("KSOPs").

  $25 for NCEO members, $35 for nonmembers

- *Employee Ownership and Corporate Performance* reviews the research that has been done on the link between company stock plans and various aspects of corporate performance.

  $25 for NCEO members, $35 for nonmembers

- *Ownership Solutions* is a 36-page booklet that discusses the various ways in which a company can share equity with its employees.

  $10 for NCEO members, $15 for nonmembers

- *Employee Ownership Concepts in Nonprofits and Government* discusses how nonprofits and governmental units, despite their lack of stock, can implement employee ownership concepts.

  $25 for NCEO members, $35 for nonmembers

- *The Journal of Employee Ownership Law and Finance* is the only professional journal solely devoted to employee ownership. Articles are written by leading experts and cover ESOPs, stock options, and related subjects in depth.

  One-year subscription (four issues):
  $75 for NCEO members, $100 for nonmembers

To join the NCEO as a member or to order any of the publications listed on the preceding pages, use the order form on the following page, use the secure ordering system on our Web site at *www.nceo.org,* or call us at 510-208-1300. If you join at the same time you order publications, you will receive the members-only publication discounts.

Order Form

To order, fill out this form and mail it with your credit card information or check to the NCEO at 1736 Franklin Street, 8th Floor, Oakland, CA, 94612; fax it with your credit card information to the NCEO at 510-272-9510; telephone us at 510-208-1300 with your credit card in hand; or order securely online at our Web site, *www.nceo.org*. If you are not already a member, you can join now to receive member discounts on publications you order.

Name

Organization

Address

City, State, Zip (Country)

Telephone   Fax   E-mail

Method of Payment: ❑ Check (payable to "NCEO") ❑ Visa ❑ M/C ❑ AMEX

Credit Card Number

Signature   Exp. Date

Checks are accepted only for orders from the U.S. and must be in U.S. currency.

Title	Qty.	Price	Total

Tax: California residents add 8.75% sales tax (on publications only, not membership or subscriptions)
Shipping: In the U.S., first publication $5, each additional $1; elsewhere, we charge actual shipping costs, plus a $10 handling fee, to your credit card; no shipping charges for membership or Journal subscriptions
Introductory NCEO Membership: $80 for one year ($90 outside the U.S.)

Subtotal	$
Sales Tax	$
Shipping	$
Membership	$
TOTAL DUE	$